*"I've been a cautious investor in the pas.
due to my lack of market knowledge and my knack for
picking the wrong investments. After using three different
financial advisors, I was introduced to Donell Smith. I liked
his straightforward approach and more importantly,
I liked the results from this approach."*
Robert Smith

---

*"I have known Captain Donell Smith since 1996. He was
instrumental in helping to establish my organization,
SHADES OF BLUE, which is helping to develop the next
generation of pilots, engineers and scientists. After the
slowing of the economy in 2007, and the huge drop in the
stock market, Captain Smith was very helpful with the
recovery of my financial portfolio. He has given sound
financial advice over the last several years, which has
allowed me to experience over 30 percent growth per year.
I have recommended several of the students involved in my
organization, to seek knowledge and financial guidance
from Captain Smith. This will allow them, at an early age,
to begin to develop their financial wealth. I congratulate
Captain on his successful endeavors and wish him many
more successful years."*
Captain Willie L. Daniels ll, President, SHADES OF BLUE

---

*"I cannot thank Donell enough for the insight, wisdom, and
direction he has provided me. After the stock market crash of
2008, my retirement account plummeted. Under his guidance,
I have watched my portfolio grow by over 300 percent, in six
years. His willingness to do research, and his knowledge and
understanding of the stock market, is second to none."*
Michael D. Dunn

"Donell Smith advised me on only one-half of my financial portfolio, and within 6 months, it had outperformed the other half of my portfolio, which was being managed by another highly recommended advisor. It outperformed the other half by 30 percent. After transferring the other half, according to Donell's educational advice, I've seen steady growth for the past 8 years. My portfolio has since passed the $1 million mark and continues to grow. Donell is always a quick phone call away with information on market changes. He is a big proponent of not getting upset when the market takes a downward turn. On the contrary, this is when Donell gets excited, for he knows it's time to BUY. I'm a true believer now. A call from Donell means it's time to make investments. Being a novice investor, Donell is always ready to explain exactly WHAT he is doing, and WHY he's making certain moves in the market. Donell is a true guru in today's markets, and as I've recommended him to countless other investors, I truly believe he has an eye for achieving financial gain."

Robert Smith, *Novice Investor*

"I was financially devastated when the company to whom I was employed declared bankruptcy. This bankruptcy lasted for over six years. My pension plan was terminated and replaced with a severely anemic Pension Benefit Guarantee Option. In desperation, I signed a costly contract with an institutional investment firm. They delivered average growth until early 2009, when the United States Stock Market fell approximately 50 percent, and my now managed pension plan was once again on life support. I tried, over the next few years, to manage my pension account, but in the end, I had miserably failed to enhance my financial future. It was

*only when a fellow co-worker and friend offered to provide
me with financial guidance and broaden my understanding
of available tools that could be used to create wealth,
that my situation improved. I will be forever grateful
to my spiritual brother, Donnell Smith, for ensuring my
financial retirement health, as well as providing me with the
knowledge and skills to further expand my wealth."*

Leon E. Miller

---

*"Having had the privilege of meeting Mr. Donell Smith
and spending a few days traveling the country, it was
quickly apparent that his passion is to bless others with
his knowledge of finances. Since January of 2019, my
retirement account went from a mere 7 percent, to a year-
to-date return of 53.5 percent. In addition, his guidance on
refinancing our home to pay off interest-bearing loans, was
simply genius. This simple fix enabled us to maximize our
retirement contributions. Now we are debt-free and on our
way to retire with the comfort of loving life. His book,
A must buy!"*

John Brennan, Pilot, United Airlines

The Common Man's Financial Guide

"Making Money Work for You"

E. Donell Smith

ENTEGRITY
CHOICE PUBLISHING

Entegrity Choice Publishing
PO Box 453
Powder Springs, GA 30127
info@entegritypublishing.com
www.entegritypublishing.com
770.727.6517

Printed in the United States of America

The views expressed in this work are solely those of the author and do not necessarily reflect the views of the publisher, and the publisher hereby disclaims any responsibility for them. The publisher is not responsible for websites (or their content) that are not owned by the publisher.

All scriptures are from the New King James Version Bible.

Library of Congress Cataloging-in-Publication Data
ISBN 978-1-7330301-2-0 (Paperback)
ISBN 978-1-7330301-5-1 (Hardcover)

Library of Congress Control Number: 2019911823

ACKNOWLEDGEMENTS

I would like to dedicate this book to my father, Henry, and Mother, Eva, for always believing in me despite humble beginnings, and for giving me my first lessons of how critical financial literacy can either make or break you. When you have "little" resources at your disposal you have to be a great steward! My mother and father both knew how to stretch a dollar, meal, and paycheck. My first lesson: "waste nothing" not even a bad experience!

This book could not have been written without the hardship and gut-wrenching anxiety of financial burdens and understanding that we don't deserve anything but judgement. Frankly speaking, we are selfish in our natural state and try to protect what we perceive as ours. In reality we are all pitiful and lost in a world determined to implode on itself due to self-focused agendas. As a child I was taught God is gracious and merciful, and He takes what others have thrown away and turns their trash into your treasure! This book was written with all the pain, passion, forethought, energy, love and dedication to those who want to live their best financial life and those wanting and needing to leave a legacy to their children and loved ones that follow. This has been an assignment of love! Please enjoy it and allow yourself the freedom to use what this great country and world offers that allows a commoner like me to become financially free despite making all the mistakes in the "do's and don'ts of the" financial bible!

TABLE OF CONTENTS

INTRODUCTION

Most people think they're above average in intelligence, relationship status and professional achievement. Social scientists call this "illusory superiority." Scott Puritz, Managing Director of Rebalance (a financial services firm), has found the one area where even above-average people, objectively smart, rich, successful professionals, seem to wave the white flag and admit to not understanding - money and investing.

"One of the most shocking things is the low-level financial literacy throughout our culture," Puritz told the Washington Post. "It's independent of education. Doctors, MBAs, corporate executives are incredibly competent in everything they do. But when it comes to investing, you run into this cauldron of mostly negative emotions, embarrassment, frustration, guilt. It leads to paralysis."

Given the risks, what do smart, rich people actually do? The key is to lower your costs, be consistent in your investment process, and of course to save enough to build a nest egg in the first place. If you can manage that, there's a solid middle ground between doing nothing and doing too much.

The sweet spot is what we call "portfolio indexing," a form of low-cost portfolio management that harnesses the stock market's propensity to rise over time and lets compounding do its magic. (Tuchman, 2019)

Financial illiteracy is infectious throughout the country; whether across social-economic backgrounds, ethnic origins, or size of your pay check, because financial literacy is not systemically taught in our current educational system.

Financial literacy covers several concepts: Time-Value-of-Money, 401Ks, 403Bs, IRAs, Debt, Risk, Student Loans, Social Security, Retirement, Estate Planning, Trusts, Savings, Investments, Insurance, Minimum Distributions, College Funds, Mortgages, Auto Loans, Compound Interest, Bonds, and Return on Investments, just to name a few. It's a lot to learn and master, so many of us rely on parents and other adults to teach us what is important to know and practice! The problem is the subtle nuances that tend to make one rich over a period of time or trap a person in the same paycheck-to-paycheck mode, generation after generation. If you don't want to be stuck in this mode and you want your children to succeed, this is the generation that must take a stand and get educated on what is important financially. You have to know the basics, and even if you don't, you have to seek professional advice from a financial advisor who puts your needs and interest above all else.

If you are not familiar with most of the concepts listed above, don't feel bad, you are in good company. According to an annual survey conducted by the TIAA Institute and the Global Financial Literacy Excellence Center (GFLEC) at George Washington University School of Business, large numbers of Americans do not have the knowledge associated with financial decisions. The study revealed that fewer than 20% of the participants in the 2018 survey could correctly answer 75% or more of the survey questions correctly. Adds Annamaria Lusardi, GFLEC academic director, "Low levels of financial literacy—not only [among] the young but also people close to retirement—show we need to step up the effort to promote financial knowledge across the entire population." (Barney, 2018)

The lack of financial knowledge continues to highlight the wealth gap in retirement as well.

According to Scott Puritz's LinkedIn page: ... the wealthiest 1% pays the lowest price for their investments and gets the best expertise. Meanwhile, hard-working Americans are paying the highest fees and getting advice from financial advisors who may not have their best interests at heart. These fees can consume up to 30% of your retirement nest egg. (Puritz, 2019)

It's amazing that this area gets little or no attention due to the lack of knowledge. It's not the idea that rich people are smarter than everyone else, but a matter of financial education, or in most cases, a financial team of experts mandated to decrease tax liabilities for a certain person or entity. In other words, if you can afford tax and financial attorneys, you will most likely pay a lot less in taxes due to their combined level of knowledge. The less you know the more you seem to pay.

What is the answer to this and other financial illiteracy examples? Simply put, "financial education!" This book will be a start, answering questions, and giving constructive advice according to the experts in the field and great business minds that I have picked and practiced through their collective written and spoken expertise. This book is just a start, an appetizer if you will allow, to a greater base of knowledge and information that will help common people like all of us who don't have the time or resources to safely navigate the treacherous waters of the financial ocean. Basic terminology used in this book will be explained within the text or can be found in the accompanying "Glossary of Terms." The many books and articles used to simplify the mounds and mounds of financial information are also included in the "References" section of the Appendix. These books along with many others are the meat and vegetables I used to eat a healthy meal and gain financial freedom. I used the information along with a formal education (MBA Finance and Accounting, Regis University

2008, MBA International Business, Regis University 2009) to manage my personal (401K) portfolio from a few thousand dollars in 2006 to almost $1.6 million in 2018. I will caveat this result with the fact that I have a generous benefits package from my employer who pays 16 percent, based on my salary, into my 401K.

Advice: Start early, be consistent, be patient, be unemotional, and seek professional help often!

Kevin O'Leary from "Shark Tank" has some simple advice for anyone who finds investing scary: Just do it. Now! (Tuchman, Kevin O'Leary ... your debts paid off by age 45, 2019)

Remember: "If you change your mindset it becomes an asset!"

I wrote this book after countless hours agonizing over why we are not financially literate. I didn't know a whole lot about finance prior to attending Regis University, but I knew that a military retirement would not sustain my way of life if I had finished 20 years in the military. I did the math and I have to admit, that being forced to live in certain places because they were affordable did not appeal to my ego or manhood. After suffering through the aftermath of 9-11, the loss of our pensions, and an overall 62 percent pay cut, the common man was broke. I wanted to share with regular folks how to avoid the pitfalls that I fell into and how they can become Common Millionaires as well.

I also would like to thank my best friend and number one supporter, my wife Yolonda, for beliving in me and for putting up with my fascination with financial literacy. Many times I forget about everything and everyone else when I start teaching about finances! It will be worth it when we are all free!

"Until now, your money has told you what to do and how much to work. Now we're going to turn that around. You'll learn to tell your money what to do and how much to work for you."
Celso Cukierkorn, Secrets of Jewish Wealth Revealed!

———— ✿ ————

CHAPTER 1

BEGINNINGS

"When you sacrifice everything for your family,
and you're committed to changing your lifestyle to secure
a better future, it is not an act of greed,
but rather an act of faith."
— **Celso Cukierkorn,** *Secrets of Jewish Wealth Revealed!*

"And we know that all things work together for good to
them that love God, to them who are the called
according to his purpose." Romans 8:28

If someone had told me a long time ago that I would write a book on financial literacy I would have called them crazy. Why would that be crazy? I grew up poor! Of course, at the time, I didn't feel poor, look poor, or ate poorly. We were just like all the other families in the neighborhood. We lived in a modest 3-bedroom home with eight people. When I was growing up in Columbus, Mississippi, I was always fascinated with numbers. What I really liked about numbers was their consistency, no matter what. I believed my family was at a minimum, lower-middle class. I lived with my mother and father, who both worked multiple jobs along with my five siblings. I was child number five, and probably received more guidance from my father than my four sisters and older brother. (This just means I got a lot more whippings (not spankings) due to my eagerness to work and play hard, i.e. rambunctiousness.) I worked very hard in school, always trying to make 100 percent on every test and assignment, so I felt entitled to play hard and as much as I liked. The over-protective nature of my parents did not agree with my plans to play hard, so I often found myself on the wrong end of a switch when I sneaked out to play with my friends.

My brother was the oldest (nine years my senior) of the children and was already in college by the time I was able to comprehend anything financial. My four sisters (various ages), didn't really show an interest in finances initially, except for shopping with our dear mother. I never understood shopping. Hours spent looking at beautiful things often too far outside our family budget to make them a reality. What I hated most, was the fact that after all the time spent looking, walking, and sorting over clothes and shoes, I would still end up with the same things I got every year: basic underwear, socks, a few pair of pants, and sneakers ($2 a pair) from our town's dollar discount store! I was never disappointed with what I received, but that it took all day and we only went home after the store manager announced the store would be closing in the next fifteen minutes. I just wanted to be at home to play not going from store to store to store, just to end up in the same place, buying the same thing as the year before!

What I didn't get at that time of my youth, was that my mother and father were teaching me valuable lessons in financial management, accountability, consistency of purpose, and the basics of wealth building by being frugal in certain areas and enjoying spending time together dreaming of the future. In other words, they were planning for uncertainty. They both had small insurance policies that were paid in full to cover burial costs and other bills upon their untimely demise. They also had excellent credit, because they always paid their bills on time. We lived well within our means and they taught us the importance of giving away ten percent of what they earned in church called a tithe. My father also told me to always pay myself by keeping at least ten cents out of every dollar I earned. The problem was they never really let me work because education came first in our household. So, in essence I never saved any money until I completed college. But it didn't matter because in my adult life all these lessons were so ingrained in me that at twenty-one, I made my first big investment. I opened an individual retirement account (an IRA in 1982) in which 50% of all monies for the first year went to the financial planner. Yeah, I know. Something about that doesn't sound quite right! After a few years and $75,000 later I began to manage the money on my own, after I found out that the investment advisor got paid whether I made money or not. About three years into the investment cycle my account was down $4200 for the year, but the fees on my account totaled $3200. I ask him, 'why did I have to pay you money, but you lost money for me this year', and he said, "That's just the way it works." I also told him I noticed a lot of buying and selling of certain stocks in my Mutual Fund that were the worst performers and seemed to cost additional fees. His response was once again, "That's just the way it works." When I told him, I was going to no longer need his services, he stated that I couldn't do that due to withdrawal fees, I told him, "Sorry, that's just the way it works!"

A recent article highlights this phenomenon:

> When it comes to investment costs, the same dynamic kicks in. If you pay 2% of your assets a

year to a mutual-fund manager or financial adviser, that's not 2% of your yearly returns. People miss this in the fine print all the time. A 2% annual charge on your total assets is a lot of money. For many investors it's thousands of dollars a year.

And it's charged whether you have a good return, or the market sells off. In fact, over time, high-fee funds can absorb essentially all of your potential gains. You take the investment risk and the managers and your adviser keep the returns. Ideally, advisers should help lower their investment costs using index products and provide truly conflict-free advice — such as how much risk to take for your personal goals, when to rebalance, and timely financial planning ideas. Meanwhile, remember to contribute to your own future through prudent, low-cost investments. That way your money will compound into a solid financial base for retirement. (Tuchman, Kevin O'Leary...your debts paid off by age 45, 2019)

One of the main reasons I wrote this book was to shed light on the great need for financial education and freedom. For this country to be the land of opportunity, it seems to only apply to a few individuals. Our educational system has failed in the area of financial education, and because of the taboo nature of money the majority of us remain in the dark about many aspects of finances! The bible states that the "Love of money is the root of all evil," (1 Timothy 6:10) but any person who has a personal relationship with God knows this only means to not make money your 'God', rather use money as a tool. The passage further states that this unhealthy love causes a person to err from their faith and afterwards, they will have to deal with many issues. In other words, placing money ahead of other important issues will cause separation, pain, and sorrow. Not only is there not a system for financial education in this country, there is a lot of mis-information due to the lack of knowledge, and so people make up what they don't know. One of my mentors, the great C. F. Lee, once said "You don't know what you don't know!" When knowledge is not present in and through a situation, inuendo, speculation, and folklore take over.

If we are going to be successful when it comes to our finances, our eyes need to be wide open, and we need to understand and be knowledgeable concerning money. Robert Kiyosaki wrote in Increase Your Financial IQ that,

Information + Education = Knowledge,

but I want to add that:

Knowledge + Action = Financial Freedom,

when it comes to finances. This is like the friend Kiyosaki mentioned that bought new golf clubs every year in an attempt to get better at golf. Each set no doubt grew more expensive each year. The problem was, the friend never bothered to pay for golf lessons to improve his game. It's like having money (i.e. winning the $100 million lottery) without the proper knowledge of finances, means you will end up where you started, just like the golfer. The golfer's game never improved and the people that won the lottery never were able to change their true circumstances and ended up broke after a few years. (Kiyosaki, 2008)

"arrogance is knowledge minus wisdom"
- Celso Cukierkorn, *Secrets of Jewish Wealth Revealed!*

I want you to be free, no matter how much money you make each year, or how smart you may or may not be. The bible says in all thy getting, get an understanding (knowledge), and make her your constant companion! *"Wisdom is the principal thing; therefore, get wisdom: and with all thy getting get understanding."* Proverbs 4:7, 19:8 So when it comes to money and finances, it's more important to have the knowledge, with the ability to act in the proper manner, rather than having large sums of money. Money can be easily lost, but with the right financial education, money can and often will be re-accumulated.

Eagles don't fly by accident, they fly because it's their passion, or in other words, if they don't fly, they die. A story in the bible brings this to light in the book of Deuteronomy. (Deuteronomy 32:11) Eagles are born to fly higher and faster than almost all other fowl, but they still have to be taught how to fly. The mother eagle stirs up the nest to make the growing eaglets jump onto the side of the nest. Because of the high winds that are usually present at the higher altitudes of the eagles' nest, the young eaglets have to flap their wings in order to stay on the nest and not get blown off. At some point the mother eagle recognizes the strength in their wings and in turn knocks the eaglets off the nest, and flies alongside them as they fall. If they don't figure it out, she takes them back to the nest and knocks them off again until they soar.

We don't take the time to do this with financial knowledge in this country, where there is more than enough to go around. The eaglets get their education while on the side of the nest, and eventually mimic their parents wing movements and flight patterns. But our children, if they don't have great role models, are left to fend for themselves and die a slow death, mired in debt, low-paying jobs, no real retirement plan, without adequate insurance, or ever setting up an emergency fund (just to name a few). As important as financial education is, our system does not automatically teach tax strategies, investment strategies, healthy debt structures, asset allocation, retirement strategies, and overall financial health. Instead, it is left up to the 'word of mouth' method of education. And because of the fear factors, and the sob stories, the mis-information, and the lack of solid experiential training, most Americans are left not knowing what to do. The system of education has to address the problem, otherwise we will continue to have people relying only on social security in their retirement years in order to survive.

According to Robert Kiyosaki:

> Financial education isn't just numbers and spreadsheets, although they're certainly a part of it. Financial education requires a solid understanding of how business and government work, (or don't work as the case may be). And it's also knowing about history, humanities and human nature, arts and science, music and mechanics, among other things. To be a whole, healthy, and well-equipped citizen requires a holistic education that focuses not just on numbers and spreadsheets but also on the soul itself.

> All education has value, and all education can be useful as you discover and fully develop your own God-given talents. As an advocate of democratic capitalism, I believe education is critical to the economic well-being of our country and is vital to continuing America's role as a shining beacon in a world that is often dark. Education is vitally

necessary if people are to realize their full potential, and it's absolutely essential if individuals are to take responsibility for their own circumstances and thrive in the economic maelstrom in which we find ourselves. (Kiyosaki, 2008)

It was only because I was baptized by financial fires (Chapter 3), that I suffered and learned the hard way, just how important financial education really is, and how financial freedom should be a goal for all of us. It's time to fight the problems of not enough money, using too much wrong credit (i.e. credit cards), inflation, tax burdens, and nothing available for retirement! So, using myself and others as an example, this book lays out the financial problems I faced, with the solutions that were attempted, and the overall education I got as a result of going through "financial hell."

It was through all these trials and tribulations that I found my purpose, my passion, and my why! I have watched and been inspired to help others overcome their fears and inadequate education on multiple financial matters. Because all this happened to me, I understand the lessons learned are as valuable as my formal MBAs from Regis University. I now want my money to work for me, as I reduce my efforts working for money!

"And we know that all things work together for good to them that love God, to them who are the called according to his purpose." **Romans 8:28**

CHAPTER 2

IT'S NOT ROCKET SCIENCE

"We attempt to be fearful when others are greedy and to be greedy only when others are fearful." - **Warren Buffett**

"Blessed are those who find wisdom, those who gain understanding." Proverbs 3:13

The strangest thing about the world of finance, is the fact most people are deathly afraid of the subject or have absolutely no ideas about it one way or another. Kevin O'Leary, of CNBC says, that interest works both ways, and in order to really give your portfolio a fighting chance, is to get out of debt by age forty-five, and that includes your mortgage. For the more affluent this is an achievable goal, but for the average person in the middle class, this goal is difficult at best. That's a key financial concept that many folks simply don't grasp. It's a rare investment that grows faster than the economy and inflation. But most debts absolutely grow faster — some much faster.

Consider a typical retirement portfolio of stocks and bonds. You might be able to get 6% or 7% a year, averaged out. Some years will be higher, some will be lower. Go with more stocks and maybe you'll make a bit more, with more ups and downs, of course.

As a pilot for a major airline, I often ask other pilots I fly with, what's their take on one financial subject or another. The majority of the time I get blank stares, or the occasional, "I don't worry about those things." Many pilots adjust their schedules in order to maximize their pay, but only nine out of ten, pay attention to what's really going on in their retirement accounts. Nor do they adjust their free time to maximize their knowledge on the subject. On the one hand, they count every penny for every minute flown, and will scream bloody murder if their pay is missing a few bucks. On the other hand, they know little about where their money is invested, what their return on investment is, how much they will have at retirement age, or their strategy while in retirement. Join the club; sounds like the majority of Americans would fit in this club.

As I took unofficial polls for non-pilots, I also found the results to be similar! On a few rare occasions, I was pleasantly surprised that a few people actually had an idea of what their accounts contained, and a few more knew their approximate return on investment (ROI).

On these occasions, I asked them how it was possible they knew what they knew. The most popular response was, a family member (i.e. a dad, mother, brother, etc.) worked in some capacity within the financial arena and had taught them the basics of financial literacy.

The conclusion of this line of questioning is that most people treated finance, especially the stock market, like it was rocket science. Many times, the rhetoric that's repeated sounds like:

a. "My friend Jimmy lost his shirt messing around in the stock market."
b. "The market is rigged."
c. "I am fine with a 6-7% gain each year, anything more is too risky."

My financial mentor had a saying; "You don't know what you don't know." Meaning if you have not been properly exposed to certain aspects of financial literacy, you will never know what is available to you. These statements uphold this premise.

The main reason people lose a large percentage their money in the stock market is due to:

- Investing in hot tips

- Investing in companies they never heard of before

- Get rich quick schemes

- Repeatedly buying high and selling low due to market sensationalism (i.e. always on the wrong side of a trade)

- Allowing emotions to rule over solid investment strategies

The market is not "rigged" as some people may think, rather the ebbs and flows of various trading styles, make it seem as such. An example would be when a large number of options' traders, short certain stocks, and the ratio of sellers is disproportionate to the number of buyers. This ratio differential puts downward pressure on the price of the stocks until the "shorts " expire. Once the short-sellers have to cover their "puts" the pressure reverses and stock prices usually rise rapidly. These fluctuations can make it seem as though someone or something is controlling the price of stocks for the benefit of a few.

According to Warren Buffett, you should dare to be bold and purchase stocks when others are afraid of the market (selling their positions) and be willing to (sell all or part of your holdings) leave the market as others buy into a rising market. This contrarian way of investing has been very good to Mr. Buffett as he has managed to maintain a healthy average compounded return of greater than 15 percent for the past twenty years. In some of those years, his company's compounded returns exceeded 22 percent. It is very difficult to hold onto a stock position when everyone else is selling and the price of the stock seems like it is in free-fall.

For instance, I purchased my first shares of Netflix at $191/ share because I witnessed my sons watching certain shows that I know we hadn't paid for. When I asked them about it, they said they were using a friend's sign-on to this new platform called Netflix (NFLX). After researching the company and reading their annual report about the company (2011), I bought 200 shares of the stock, approximately $38,000. A few months later the stock price climbed to $295/share, wow! My $38,000 initial investment had grown to $295/share and my shares were now worth $59,000, a 55 percent gain. That was great but shortly thereafter the price plummeted due to an announcement by the CEO that NFLX would now charge separately for the streaming platform and the monthly mail subscription (overall cost would increase for those who used both). Of course, the media talked about it for several days with the consensus being the stock price would suffer due this announcement. The self-fulfilling prophecy came true and the price of the stock sunk to $63.84/share. I saw my value in NFLX drop to $12,768, a decrease of 66 percent. I couldn't believe my luck (a lot of people sold their stock as the price dropped), but I decided to take advantage of the drop and purchased additional shares of the stock at this new low price, more than doubling my overall holdings to 400 shares. By doing this I also lowered my cost basis to around $124/share from my original purchase of $191/share. Over the next four years the share price for NFLX rose towards $800/share as the company grew globally. On July 15, 2015, the stock split 1:7, and the rest of the story shows that NFLX became the darling of Wallstreet and continued its meteoric rise, dominating all other streaming services being offered. The stock then rose from the split price of $100/share to over $400 a share.

Shortly after the split, several other companies such as HBO and CBS announced their intentions to launch streaming platforms (although their launches were a full two years away). Because of this, the pundits (television personalities with varied opinions) on TV started pontificating about the downfall of Netflix and the loss of market share; the price of the stock once again dropped to historic lows of approximately $81.00/share. I once again bought more NFLX and watched my portfolio grow at an amazing rate. NFLX is what one in the industry calls a "GAME CHANGER."

As of the writing of this book, other networks and entities have started streaming services to gain a piece of the pie: Amazon Prime, Disney (11/2019), CBS, Hulu, AT&T, and Apple TV (fall/2019) to name a few. The pundits once again are talking about the downgrading of NFLX due to competition, but what they are not stressing is the fact that none of the other services have a world-wide foothold like Netflix. As a matter of fact, when I travel to other countries, I can watch shows from Hulu, Amazon Prime, and other services through

Netflix. This is because Netflix already has agreements in place all over the world except Mainland China, Syria, North Korea, and Crimea.

Every time the price of Netflix dropped it was similar to buying your adult beverage for less than half price at the grocery store, only to have the total supply to diminish causing your supply to now demand ten times the amount you paid for it. Warren Buffet and Netflix both made a believer out of me that long-term investing with a great company is a sure-fire way to get rich over time. In the case of NFLX it only took ten years to go from $38,000 to over $1.1 million with the same stock. My average return for NFLX was 40.26 percent compounded annually for ten years. Other people that got in at the beginning realized a greater than 36,000% return overall because they could have purchased 6,960 shares at ~$0.78/ share for that same $38,000. That equates to a greater than 43.48 percent average compounded return for the past seventeen years. This equates to over $17.5 million after seventeen years. The secret was to understand the company, where it was going, and that it was definitely a "game changer!" By the way, do you still see a Blockbuster Video store in every strip mall you past? That's right, NFLX changed everything, and continues to do so! There are a lot of companies that continue to change and reshape the way we live our lives; you just have to keep your eyes open. If the price of NFLX drops again, I will continue to buy more shares and add them to my portfolio until another game changer takes their place.

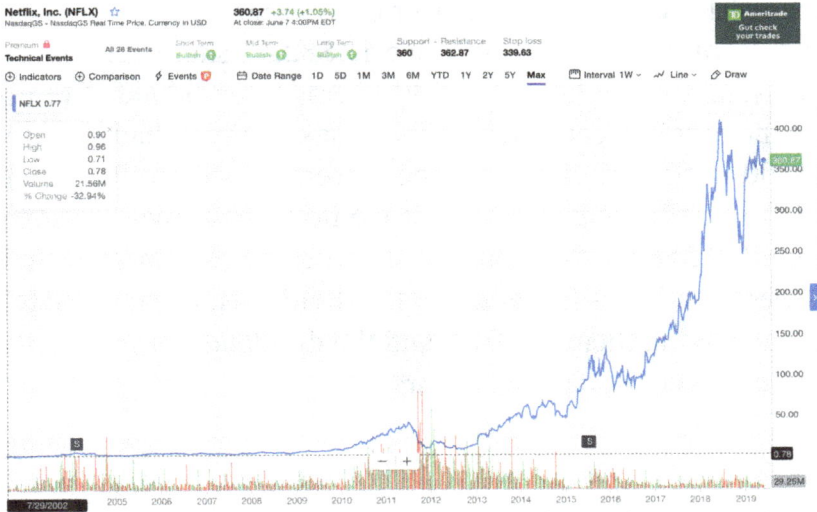

(Chart IQ, 2019)

Does this sound like "rocket science" to you? I hope not, because you can do the same thing I did, just by paying attention to a few things around you. I purchased stock in Netflix late, but that fact did not deter me from sticking with it! Over the past eleven years my continued investment in NFLX has gained an additional $300,000.

When I drive or walk by a Starbucks (SBUX), I see a long line and people patiently waiting to spend $5-9.00 a day on a cup of coffee and a pastry or sandwich. You may think this phenomenon is only in the morning, but I assure you the lines can be as long at the lunch hour as well as the hours immediately after the workday ends. I have also seen long lines at night as people gather to socialize over a cup of coffee, study college subjects, or discuss the day's events with colleagues. So, to decide to invest in Starbucks is no more complicated than understanding what you are seeing with your eyes and believing what you see. Starbucks was and still is a game changer! It's split adjusted price was $0.36/share in 1992 and as of June 2019, the price is $82.48/share; giving the savvy investor a healthy 22.30 average compounded return for the past 27 years. What this means is; if you had invested $1000 in SBUX in 1992 when it went on sale to the public (IPO-initial public offering), it would have grown to a measly $229,358.00. Not bad for the average person who likes coffee! Let's not forget about the dividends, because SBUX began paying them in 2010, and the dividend has grown 300 percent over the past nine years.

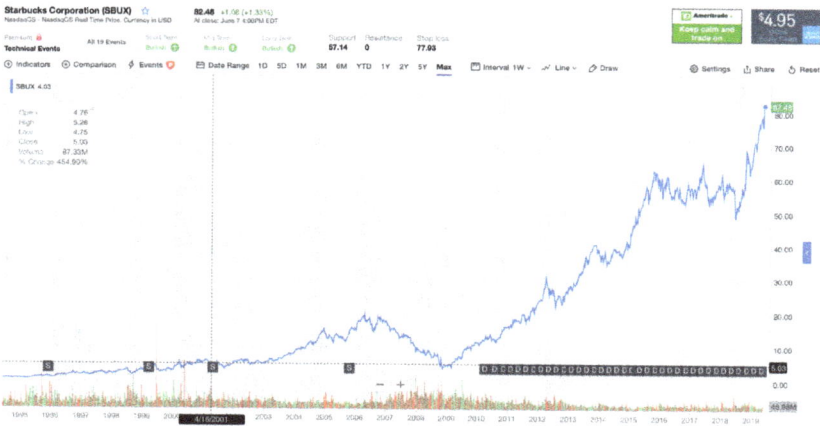

(Chart IQ, 2019)

So, it's really not complicated like you have heard, or you may suspect. But it is a matter of paying attention to what is going on around you every day. For instance, when did braces become clear, and when did orthodontists start straightening teeth using clear trays versus those embarrassing braces that children hate to wear for two years at a time? If you had noticed the trend and further noticed that the trend was the new thing in all areas of the world, you would have probably purchased stock with Align Technologies (ALGN), the maker and first company to market and sell invisible trays to straighten teeth. In 2001 you could have purchased the stock at $6.81 and today that same stock is selling at $331.08/share, a 24.08 percent average return compounded annually. This means that a $1000 investment in ALGN in 2001 would have grown to $48,599.00 after only eighteen years.

(Chart IQ, 2019)

Single digit gains in the 6-8 percent range are fine, as long as your portfolio doesn't lose in direct proportion to market corrections. In other words, if your portfolio moves down-ward with the market, a 10-15 percentage correction on the downside, will cause your portfolio to decrease in proportion until the market manages to rebound to previous levels. It took approximately twelve to eighteen months for the market to rebound during the financial crises of 2008. During their time of decrease, it is either best to just hold what you have until the markets bottom out or the more aggressive investors buy during the downturn, purchasing more shares until the price hits rock bottom. Although this sounds risky on the surface, in reality it is a great strategy to increase your number of stocks, lower you cost basis, and reap the benefits of a greater dividend ratio due to the lower price of the stock. This strategy works best for companies that are strong, with great financials, and will be around for the long term.

Other stocks that are household names that are considered strong companies are names like: Nike, Home Depot, Lowes, Walmart, McDonalds, Amazon, Google, Walt Disney, Visa, Mastercard, Auto Zone, and Federal Express- to name a few! Just look around you, for what your children are asking for, what your neighbors are buying, and what your spouse is doing. Usually these are simple yet proven techniques that indicate where we are headed, and which companies are poised to take us there. On the other hand, you could watch the experts/pundits on television for the answers.

When you watch CNBC, MSNBC or other financial channels, it sounds like the commentators are speaking a foreign language (i.e. "rocket science") because of the terms used on the various financial channels. With a little review and some practice with terms such as, "basis points," options, bonds, premiums, discounts, IPOs, long, short, buybacks, etc.; these terms and others will become a part of your everyday vocabulary.

At the end of the day, a couple of things make a portfolio work.

- Buying stock in great companies (world-wide and financially secure, and well-run).

- Consistency in making stock purchases (make purchases each month if you can).

- The best time to buy is usually during bad news either

with the company, the entire market, or just a particular sector of the market.

- Time is your friend. By allowing compound interest to work for you, it will take less time for your portfolio to build up.

- Diversity across all investment sectors and stock betas (Beta is a measure of a stock's volatility in relation to the overall market or as measured against the S&P 500 index).

- If the market takes a rapid down turn, use it as an opportunity to increase positions in your favorite holdings.

- If the market stays down for a while (say greater than 4 months), increase your positions in dividend paying stocks and continue to purchase the great companies you already own.

Historically the market increases over time. If you look at a 40-year chart of any of the major indexes (NYSE, S&P500, NASDQ, or DOW), you will see ups and downs in the market over the short term, but a gradual increase over any five, ten, fifteen, or twenty year period.

Let's look at a typical investment of $250.00 per month, invested over a 30-year period, at 10 compounded interest. (See chart to the right.)

Principal Amount	**250**
Monthly Deposit	**250**
Period (month)	**360**
Annual Interest Rate%	**10**
Compounding	Monthly
Reset	Calculate
Total Principal:	90,250.00
Interest Amount:	484,540.69
Maturity Value:	574,790.68
APY:	10.4713%

The result would be a nice ending value of $574,790.68. Most people in the US retire with less than $200,000.00 in the bank. So, you can see with a little consistency and long-term goals, a half million-dollar retirement is not out of reach.

Most people never think this is possible due to all the reasons mentioned above. With a little education, forethought, and consistency this would be totally possible. There are also some mutual funds that have been averaging constantly over 10 percent per year for the past ten years. From Kiplinger. com the list includes: Fidelity Advisor Growth (FAGAX), Morgan Stanley Multi-Cap Growth A (CPOAX), Eaton Vance-Atlanta Capital Focused Growth (EAALX), Calvert Social Investment Equity Portfolio A (CSIEX), Franklin Templeton Dyna Tech A (FKDNX), Artisan Thematic Inv (ARTTX), and Ridge Worth Aggressive Growth Stock A (SAGAX), to name a few. (Morning Star, Inc, 2019)

If we could manage to increase the interest rate towards what Warren Buffett normally gets, the returns increase significantly! Warren Buffett's average return has been between 15-20 percent for several years. If you could manage a 15 percent average return (most financial advisors would consider this risky, if not impossible). Your returns would grow significantly. (Hagstrom, 2005)

"We attempt to be fearful when others are greedy and to be greedy only when others are fearful." -**Warren Buffett**

Principal Amount   **250**

Monthly Deposit   **250**

Period (month)   **360**

Annual Interest Rate%   **15**

Compounding   Monthly

Reset   Calculate

Total Principal: **90,250.00**
Interest Amount: **1,684,090.38**
Maturity Value: **1,774,340.40**
APY: **16.0755%**

Just an additional 5 percent would increase the ending value to just over $1.77 million dollars after 30 years. So, just $250 invested consistently over time will work, you just have to continue to not be afraid of downturns, don't get too excited about upswings. One of the keys to investing is to take the emotions out of investing and just do it!

If you decided to double your contribution to $500 per month, your overall value would then double to $3.5 million. This amount of money has the potential to set you free of money problems and burdens for the rest of your life. (See chart to the right)

< Home   **Compound Interest** Advanced

Principal Amount   **500**

Monthly Deposit   **500**

Period (month)   **360**

Annual Interest Rate%   **15**

Compounding   Monthly

Reset   Calculate

Total Principal: **180,500.00**
Interest Amount: **3,368,180.75**
Maturity Value: **3,548,680.80**
APY: **16.0755%**

In order to figure out these numbers I suggest using a financial calculator app called EzCalculators. ($4.95 from the app store). There are approximately 50 different calculators for your personal use. Never get surprised again by numbers you don't understand. Theses calculators allow you to easily run all financial calculations that you will probably ever need.

Menu   **fncalculator.com** Search Edit

TVM Calculator	Currency Converter	Loan Calculator	Compound Interest Calc...
Retirement/ 401k Calcul...	Tip Calculator	APR Calculator	ROI Calculator
Auto Loan Calculator	Auto Lease Calculator	Credit Card Payoff Calcu...	Credit Card Minimum Pa...
Discount and Tax Calculator	IRR NPV Calculator	Calculator	Percentage Calculator
Bond Calculator	Stock Calculator	Miscellaneous Calculators	

CHAPTER 3

BAPTISM BY FIRE

"Someone's sitting in the shade today because someone planted a tree a long time ago." -**Warren Buffett**

"As long as the earth endures, seedtime and harvest, cold and heat, summer and winter, day and night will never cease." *Genesis 8:22*

There's nothing like a cold bucket of water being poured over your head to wake you up. If you don't drown, all of your senses are on fire and your brain is in overdrive to process what just happened.

Everything was going along fine or so I thought, until my marriage ended in divorce. Not only that, but 9-11 took place not long after that and it seemed the world that I once knew, was in shambles around my feet. Our airline declared bankruptcy, and a few months later the pilots took a 62 percent pay cut, along with loss of position, medical insurance costs increased by 30 percent, and we furloughed thousands of pilots.

"It was like waking up in a mental, psychological, and financial nightmare...."

My self-esteem was in the proverbial toilet, and my finances were shot. Although I had saved and planned for the future, theses well-timed tragedies had the profound effect of launching me into a state of depression. It was so bad, that my doctor was shocked to hear of all the mishaps. He stated, "How have you not had a mental breakdown." He sent me to an analyst who administered a stress test. My score was 500 out of a possible 315. I was in dangerous territory.

After the divorce I had exactly $7000 in my 401K account. Our ESOP (Employee-owned Stock Ownership Plan) stock had fallen in price from a high of $200/share to only a measly $1.00/share. Instead of receiving $880,000, I only got $4400 for my 4400 shares. By the way, my debts due to the divorce and credit card purchases (we lived on credit cards to keep up appearances) had blossomed to $84,000.

A few months later with the encouragement of a friend, I decided to pursue an MBA in Finance and Accounting because of the uncertainty of my chosen profession. By immersing myself into the world of finance I was able to find my true calling. Many people go through life without ever discovering what that is for them. I loved everything about finance especially the numbers and the relationship between numbers. I realized that with a few facts, a regular person like me could in fact, evaluate a business and offer suggestions for improvement (with a little practice and guidance of course). Being in school had quenched my baptismal fire and I started to live again, go out again, and enjoy life.

But as the saying goes, "When it rains, it pours!" Soon after the break up of my marriage, my older son began to have bouts of depression, due to his best friend's suicide. Our son was extremely bright and had tested in the lower genius range as far as his IQ was concerned. His results had put him solidly in genius territory with a 153 rating. I on the other hand had only tested at a 133 rating.

Lewis Terman (1916) developed the original notion of IQ and proposed this scale for classifying IQ scores:

- Over 140 - Genius or near genius

- 120 - 140 - Very superior intelligence

- 110 - 119 - Superior intelligence

- 90 - 109 - Normal or average intelligence

- 80 - 89 - Dullness

- 70 - 79 - Borderline deficiency

- Under 70 - Definite feeble-mindedness

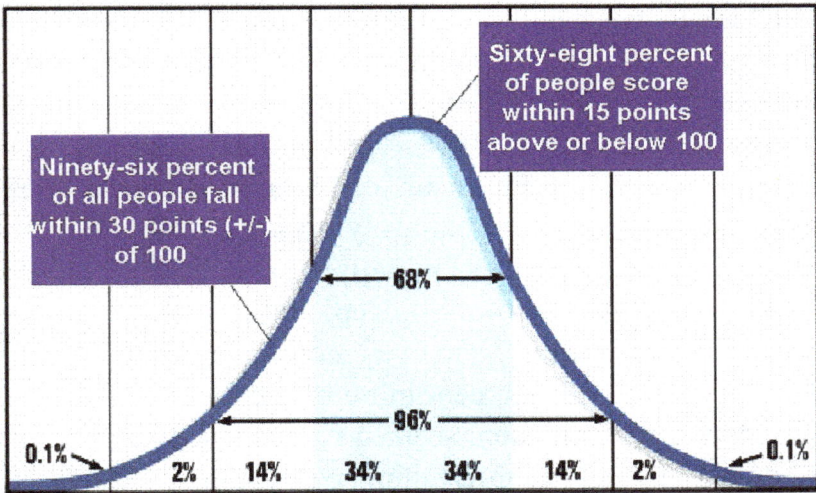

(Key Players in the History & Development of Intelligence & Testing, 2005)

Although my son had scored in the upper level of the chart, he was so hurt and confused by the events in his life that he developed affective-schizoid disorder! This meant several trips to hospitals, counselors, doctors, emergency rooms, specialists, and eventually residential treatment. It was a tough time; tears and prayer often accompanied each other in my bed at night.

In the meantime my 14-yar old daughter, started dating without our knowledge and caused quite a stir when she disappeared one night at between 1:00 am and 3:00 am. As smart as she was, she had turned to her now boyfriend for stability as the divorce continued to wreak havoc on all of us. We found her without incident, after getting the police involved, and after a 2-hour search of the neighborhood, sitting in the park with her boyfriend. It was 32-degrees and neither one of them had on a coat. They were shivering and extremely cold! Our daughter said she just wanted to spend some time with him, and he had come over to the house in the middle of the night to ask her to meet him outside. These events were just the tip of the iceberg of what seemed like hell on earth.

So, not only did I have to go to school at night, work 10 hours a day, hospital visits, cook, help with homework, and clean the house; our company declared bankruptcy and cut our pay by 30 percent, initially! I say initially because eventually the pay cut was so deep, that it settled at a solid 62 percent cut in salary, and even more in benefits. Eventually, I had to pay 30 percent more of the medical bills out-of-pocket. Bill collectors seemed to literally, line up at my front door, with letters threatening legal action if I didn't pay. A snow storm caused damage to my downstairs neighbor's condo unit, which was blamed on me because I didn't shovel off my patio. I was up to my @## in alligators. On top of all of that, the company decided to furlough another 1500 pilots, and although I had enough seniority to remain, I lost my Captain's seat and had to go back to being a co-pilot. This move cost me another 20-30 percent cut in pay. By this time, I had lost count, and my only indicator of how bad it had gotten, was the fact that I often flew my 3-day trips to Hawaii with only $20-25 in my wallet and no room on the credit cards.

Any assets that had been available to me, 401K, home equity, or loans had been frozen by the divorce judge. I was being accused of trying to hide assets, of which I had very little, and not living up to my obligations to my estranged spouse for support! Not only that, but the opposition lawyer petitioned the court and received a garnishment of my check, before I ever got a cent from my work.

Making a decision to not give up or give into the pressures of life is the first step on the road to recovery. You have to know that bad times don't always last, and God loves his children and has plans in place for them. I refused to become a victim of my devastation to my family, to my job, and to my financial situation. I pushed depression out of my mind and took a stand to move forward one step at a time!

CHAPTER 4

STARTING OVER

"College graduates spent 16 years gaining skills that will help them command a higher salary; yet little or no time is spent helping them save, invest and grow their money."
– **Vince Shorb, CEO, National Financial Educators Council**

"Wilt thou not revive us again: that thy people may rejoice in thee?" Psalm 85:6

How do you start over from devastating financial suicide? How can you see a solution when all you see are bills, bills, and more bills? I still remember calling each utility company, phone company, credit card company, and furniture store to ask for a more favorable payment plan based on my current income and debt obligations. You begin by getting up each day and pressing towards a goal with set milestones enroute to the overall goal. With only $7000 in my 401K, $84,000 in debt, child support payments, and a 62 percent pay cut, I was not ready to face the world, but I had to. It wasn't about me now. It was about my children. It was about anyone who worked for me at the office. (I had taken a pilot management job at the training center for our airline in order to be home for the kids.) It was about the future generation that was coming behind me. Of course, these thoughts were not in my immediate mind, but just below the surface. I knew if I just held fast, things would get better. Little did I know the overall condition would last almost 10 years.

My first order of business was to get in shape physically and seek counseling for my own and my children's emotional distress! So, I joined a local gym approximately one mile from my condo and sought professional counseling for myself and my children. Next, I enrolled in Regis University located in the north part of Denver and attended Regis Monday through Thursday nights. Because my management job ended, I went back to flying weekly trips Friday through Monday. So, I had a full schedule Monday – Sunday, and maintained that pace for three years.

I prayed a lot and continued to teach adult Sunday School at my church, in spite of the difficult times I was going through. Because of counseling and having great friends at work and church, I made it through the toughest part of my life. I kept my head down and pressed toward the goals I had set for myself. Since 9-11 had just happened, and the fate of my airline was still in jeopardy, my first goal was to shop my MBA for a job on Wallstreet. As I was finishing my first MBA, Wallstreet began laying off over 20,000 investment bankers and financial personnel. So, I decided to get a second MBA in international business, by taking credits from the first MBA (Finance and Accounting), and using them as prerequisites towards the second MBA (International Business). I applied to several job websites to shop my newly honed skills, and because the housing crises had begun a few months earlier (Fall 2007), I never got any offers. I even hired a head hunter to help me get placed; I was going to take a sabbatical from my airline until things improved. I never got a call!

So, I decided to not focus on what I didn't have, but to focus on what I did have. I had not one but 2 MBAs, and I still had a job that was now contributing 16 percent to my 401K (although at a 62 percent pay cut). Also, I had taken as many elective courses as possible in portfolio management and banking. So, I had a solid idea of how to manage a portfolio, but not a great education on how to choose the best companies to invest in based on the information provided on any financial websites. All my life I had been a reader, and I had read and learned about Warren Buffett, Lee Iacocca, and Peter Lynch, Patrick A. Lyons, Tony Robbins, T. Harv Ecker, and Robert Kiyosaki. Because I loved to read, I decided to read the books from those who had done it before.

But it was while reading the biographies and the "how to" books written by these great men, that I really learned. Not so much from statistical or mathematical sense, but a common sense. These books are written in an easy and common-sense way that anyone can use to choose great companies to invest in. One of theories that had the most impact on me was the idea to buy companies that were undervalued by the masses and the gurus of Wallstreet. According to Peter Lynch, author of Beating the Street and former manager of the Magellan Fund, he bought companies that were more and more under-valued than his previous purchases. He states:

> Rather than being constantly on the defensive, buying stocks and then thinking of new excuses for holding on to them if they weren't doing well (a great deal of energy on Wall Street is still devoted to the art of concocting excuses), I tried to stay on the offensive, searching for better opportunities in companies that were more undervalued than the ones I'd

chosen. In 1979, a good year for stocks in general, Magellan was up 51 percent while the S&P rose 18.44 percent. In the annual report to shareholders, once again I faced the challenge of explaining my strategy, as if I had one to begin with. "Increased holdings in lodging, fast-food restaurants, and retail" was the best I could do. (Lynch, 1993)

So, instead of picking just the hot stocks and suffering like the other experts on Wall Street, Lynch picked companies whose stock price had been depressed or pushed down but had potential to grow and display their true value. This premise along with Warren Buffett's plan to squeeze a nickel out of undervalued companies, made me realize that investing in great companies that had a quarter or two of bad news, may in fact become undervalued and attractive long-term investments. So, armed with my newly motivate state of mind, I was ready to walk out of the fire and into the world of investing. I was back to feeling like myself again. What I found quite by accident was stocks whose prices had appreciated over 1000 percent over a ten-year period. The first company I found was Popeyes Louisiana Chicken, after witnessing a line of cars going around the block, just waiting to purchase that delectable spice-infused chicken. It started as a trickle but soon built up into a raging river. If Popeyes can have a great stock, then this could apply to other companies as well. After doing some more research, I found over 30 companies whose historical stock prices had risen >1000% over the previous ten years. I thought, why buy mutual funds (average returns of 6-8%), when other equities can deliver >30% compound interest per year! The most interesting thing of all, was the theories that Buffett, Lynch, and Ecker touted, were confirmed. It's not rocket science, just math, you just have to pay attention to what's being bought or sold around you. The companies were all house-hold names, with few exceptions. It's what the young women are buying, what your spouse and their friends are into, what the kids are all raving about, and what the neighbors can't seem to get enough of. Some of the stocks I found were Apple (AAPL), Starbucks (SBUX), Nike (NKE), and Chipotle (CMG) just to name a few.

The key trigger point was what was witnessed versus what the financials showed. You can see the long lines at Starbucks, the endless line of people going to Chipotle, and the thousands of people willing to pay $270-1000.00 for a unique pair of Nikes. People sometimes buy a company's stock based on a hot tip (not recommended), research into its financials, proven staying power, or momentum. But what I found was all of these things are needed to help make a decision, but the most important was the companies that introduced new products and services that actually impacted the way we lived and interact with others. In other words, "game-changers" are the companies that make the difference in our lives and eventually our investments.

In the past all I heard was diversify, diversify, diversify, which on the surface seems smart and conservative. It is what we call in the industry the modern portfolio theory. But the reason for that diversification is to mitigate fluctuations in the prices of your stock holdings. According to Warren Buffett, too much diversification, leads to mediocrity. He believes, as do I, that purchasing a few outstanding companies that have a sensible price and have a proven advantage over their competitors, is the quintessential key to low-risk investing. He goes on further to say:

> "If you are a know-nothing investor, able to under-
> stand business economics and to find five to ten

sensibly priced companies that possess important long-term competitive advantages, conventional diversification (broadly based active portfolio) makes no sense for you." (Hagstrom R. G., 2005)

Now, that strategy to buy mutual funds due to their diversification seems a bit outdated. Initially, the idea was to allow the small investor to participate in the world of high finance without having to pay a big price, but systematically over time they could reap great benefits of purchasing partial shares of several different companies at a low entry price per month. Eventually, the fund managers and owners of the mutual funds continued to add fees with any and all costs passed on to the clients. But the biggest problem is neither the financial advisors, the fund managers, nor the fund administrators who were fiduciaries for the client. The problem is, the firm makes money whether the small-time investor makes any money at all, or even if they lose money. In other words, nobody is looking out for the little guy! The way to rectify the situation was to make sure as many people as possible understood the basics of finance and investing, and to provide as much direction, education, and insight as requested.

In his book "The Warren Buffett Way," Hagstrom gives us the rules of investing:

The Focus Investor's Golden Rules

1. Concentrate your investments in outstanding companies run by strong management.

2. Limit yourself to the number of companies you can truly understand. Ten to twenty is good, more than twenty is asking for trouble.

3. Pick the very best of your good companies and put the bulk of your investment there.

4. Think long-term: five to ten years.

5. Volatility happens: Carry on.

(Hagstrom R. G., 2005)

So, when I began to really invest in 2009, the market was coming off an extremely poor year, laced and riddled with the bullets of a defunct housing market, rising national debt, high unemployment, and a crippled financial industry. It was the perfect time for me to invest, as a self-proclaimed contrarian investor, the super low stock prices were exactly what I needed to get started. Because the entire market had suffered a meltdown, everything was on sale, and because I didn't have much to invest at the time, I knew the market would recover over time and my portfolio would bare the fruits of its recovery. I was armed with knowledge and I was ready! I still wasn't very happy though because of all that I had gone through. With my faith intact and oozing with the influence of the financial sages, I felt like I could once again face the world on my own terms.

I had been given a gift and a second chance; I was not about to waste either. Sometimes all you need is a chance!

CHAPTER 5

WHY FINANCIAL FREEDOM

"The world always pays you less than you are worth.
Don't sell yourself short even further."
– Celso Cukierkorn, **Secrets of Jewish Wealth Revealed!**

"A good person leaves an inheritance for their children's
children…" **Proverbs 13:22**

At this point in my life I was just upset and mad at the world, the justice system, my former spouse, the business world, and all the managers that were paid 1000 percent more than their median-salaried workers. Our company had filed for and was granted bankruptcy (2006), thereby negating long standing contracts, pensions, creditors, medical coverage, work rules, and numerous other employee and vendor related issues. I found myself living pay-check to pay-check but ends never met. I fell further and further behind on all my bills and became more and more depressed, although I didn't realize my condition until I was on my way out. So, with all the financial pressures ($84,000 in debt, child and maintenance support payments, a 62 percent reduction in salary, and loss of pension) and the uncertainty of job security I was anything but financially free. I felt like I was in a never-ending story of trial and tribulations. All my life I had worked hard to do the right things, the right jobs, excel at every level, but once again life handed me lemons. At this point, I didn't know how to make lemonade. So, I went back to school, worked hard at my church, and volunteered to teach young people about aviation, aerospace, and all components of STEM through a non-profit that I was instrumental in creating (Shades of Blue: ourshadesofblue.org). What I needed was financial freedom, but a job didn't seem to have what I needed to make that happen.

How should we define financial freedom? According to western culture, financial freedom is the ability to live within one's means for the rest of your life without working for a wage or salary. In other words, you are no longer working for your money, it now works for you!

Stress Relief

The first benefit of financial freedom in my personal experience was stress relief.... When you don't have to worry about stealing from Peter to pay Paul, it's a relief... just being able to pay your bills on time, the thought of getting the plumbing fixed as soon as it breaks, it's a relief... Or if you have ever had a bill collector call you and say nicely that you are behind on your payment to them and they need to know when you plan on paying your bill. They even give you payment plans to catch up if you can't pay it all at once, will also relieve some additional pressure.

Economic Power

It's really an unfortunate fact that financial illiteracy is an epidemic in our nation that is based in the premise of capitalism. The problem seems to be in the lack of an emphasis on any type of financial education, beyond balancing a check-book, paying bills, and having a few thousand dollars saved in the bank. Having met these goals your economic power is nil. You can vote but you usually feel powerless to make any significant changes in your neighborhood or city!

You usually don't participate in politics or in the planning for your surrounding sphere of influence. As a matter of fact, you don't feel as though you have any influence at all.

On the other have, if you had significant resources, you would automatically feel more empowered. People at higher pay scales/middle class tend to vote more often and partici-pate in community events and activities.

Retirement

Trying to retire on social security benefits alone seems extremely daunting. If you had no freedom or power prior to retirement, you definitely will fare worse in retirement!

Financial freedom allows those who have properly saved and invested to reap the blessings of relaxation, great health benefits, travel, recreation, and philanthropy. It's like the "Red Bull" commercial. "Financial freedom gives you wings!"

Solves Problems

I know a lot of people who rather fix items that are broken around the house themselves. Some projects take days weeks and some months. I have found that I get great satisfaction freeing up that time to spend it with my family, or taking on a more mentally challenging task, than building a deck, lay-ing sod, or mowing the lawn. When I was younger, I did all these tasks and really enjoyed the feeling of accomplishment. As I got older my priorities changed and "work-life balance" became a buzz word and a priority. So now, I would rather let my money do those tasks for me, and I can spend that time where it really matters, with my family!

Saves Money

The best benefit of Financial Freedom is it saves money. Having bills under control, and large sums of money in the bank equate to much higher credit scores. This in turn means lower interest rates on real estate loans, business loans, auto loans, and personal loans. It also means lower rates on lines of credit, credit cards, and fees associated with start-up utilities when you move into a new residence. Over a long period of time these savings add up. Some experts estimate $1,000,000 savings over a life time, based on a great credit score. The question becomes what can you do with an extra million dollars? Financial freedom is just the beginning. In the end it gives you options.

Creates Legacy

What better way to honor what gifts God has given you, than by leaving a legacy for your children and their children? What you start and teach to your children inevitability will be passed on to future generations to come. Isn't it our task to leave the world a better place for our children than it was for us? I'm not totally sure about this information, but it was explained to me by a friend that was very close to a Jewish family in Atlanta, that in this family, the grandparents always left $1 million insurance policies to the grandchildren to fund their futures. So, if you don't want money for you, you can always give it to those in need. You can leave it for educational purposes, to create equality and a chance for those less fortunate to change their lives for the better!

CHAPTER 6

FIRST THINGS FIRST

"There are just three things that you can do with Money: save, give, or invest. Somehow in here in America, with all our creativity, we have invented a fourth use for money: we can squander it."
– *Celso Cukierkorn,* **Secrets of Jewish Wealth Revealed!**

"Well then, you should have put my money on deposit with the bankers, so that when I returned, I would have received it back with interest." Matthew 25:27

There is an old saying that goes pay yourself first. If you pay everyone else; bills, children, charity, and banks, please don't forget about you! There is a time and season for everything, and this is the season to get out of debt, stay out of debt, and to allow your money to work for you. In order for your money to work for you, you have to have money, and you will have to be consistent in adding money to the total to take advantage of the ups and the downs while investing.

Develop an Emergency Fund

I agree with the experts concerning the importance of

having an emergency fund equal to three to six months living expenses. This money has to be fairly liquid, and easily accessible, but it doesn't have to necessarily have to be in a savings account. There are several investment accounts that issue checks and debit cards giving you instant access to your funds. If all your cash is fully invested, you will have to sell some of stocks in order to withdraw funds. It usually takes two to three days for funds to clear after the sale of stock. So, if you need the money quickly, you will have to keep cash in the money market portion of the account for easier accessibility.

Setting up an emergency fund is critical to avoid using credit cards when problems arise. It could be as simple as an unexpected auto repair or having to replace a washer and dryer. Having an account to withdraw funds whether planned or unplanned will give you and your family peace of mind. You have to be disciplined and determined to put this in place to avoid the temptation to overuse credit or withdraw funds from a retirement account.

One of the benefits of having your emergency fund in an investment account is the potential for growth. If you do not use the funds in the account for a few months, they will accumulate more shares through dividends or growth. With credit card interest rates ranging from 18-26 percent, you will definitely be better off financially not using them unless you have the discipline to pay them in full every month.

Pay Down or Refinance Debt

If you find yourself in some credit card debt, falling behind on bills, and not able to get ahead, you may consider a few options to get back on the right track. One way would be to borrow money from yourself. Some 401K accounts allow you to take a loan out from your retirement account and pay it back in installments over a few years (usually a maximum of 5 years). Using your 401K allows you to pay off the credit cards, get a head start on your emergency fund, and catch up on any delinquent bills without incurring additional debt. As a matter-of-fact, your monthly income versus out flow should increase due to the credit cards being paid off.

By taking the necessary steps above you have effectively:

1. Stopped paying huge interest in money you have already spent.
2. Improved your credit score.
3. Began paying yourself interest on the loan you made to yourself.
4. Started an emergency fund to avoid future debts and increased interest payments.
5. Put yourself in a position to win financially.
6. Increased the amount of money remaining after bills have been paid.
7. Began paying yourself first.

Another way to achieve this is to refinance a home or property that has some equity. Essentially equity is the difference between what you owe on a property/house and what the property is worth. Banks and lending institutions will lend up to 80-90 percent of the value of a home which allows you to get cash out of the equity portion to pay bills, eliminate credit card debt, and start an emergency fund. This process is more involved and requires you to have a great credit score, usually in the 720-800 range in order to get the loan. Some lending institutions will consider credit scores as low as 630. By using money from the refinance (cash out), you will effectively:

1. Lower your taxable income

2. Increase your cash inflows

3. Build an emergency fund

4. Increase your peace of mind

5. Roll the money from your revolving accounts and credit cards into a tax-deductible instrument

As I consult with families, and I find a discrepancy between the husband and wife in terms of financially literacy, a financial crisis is usually looming. If you choose either of these options both spouses must be disciplined and agree/buy-into the financial plan. Otherwise, you will find yourself worse than before if you go back into debt.

How Does This Look in Practice?

Mark and Susan have combined incomes totaling $135,000. They have three credit cards with a total debt of $40,000 and they are paying $1000/month in car payments. Their mortgage is $1500/month (including taxes and insurance) and they are expecting a baby girl in three months. Their combined student loan debt is $90,000 with a monthly payment of $500. Because they pay their bills on-time they have credit scores averaging 750 points. When the baby arrives, Susan will stay home thereby reducing their overall income by $55,000. Since they have been in their home over seven years, Mark and Susan have built up some equity in their home and it is accessible to them if they qualify based on their credit score, income level, debt level, and specifically their history of mortgage payments. They are concerned with the addition of the baby and a decrease of income; they will struggle to have any extra money to enjoy life.

They realize they need to eliminate debt until Susan returns to work. In order to do so they opted to use the equity value in their home. After meeting with a financial advisor, they found the following information. Their home was worth $275,000, which they had purchased several years earlier for $165,000. Currently they only owed $110,000 This meant their equity was $165,000 and with loan to value ratios at 80 percent, they would be able to borrow $110,000 from the equity in their house. Using this money, they could eliminate the high-interest credit card debt, pay off the cars ($25,000 remaining to be paid), and have over $45,000 left over to pay down the student loan debt and use some funds to get the house ready to receive the new baby.

Old outflow of cash monthly: $3000 (Old Mortgage + Cars + Student Loans)

New out flow after re-finance monthly: $1950 (New Mortgage + ½ Student Loan Payment)

With the new baby Mark and Susan will have more deductions to their taxes and pay a lot less towards taxes each month due to the loss of income. With the new funds they will be able to financially weather the storm of having Susan home with the new bundle of joy!

Maximize Your Credit Score

There are several high-quality credit restoration/building services available today. By paying a low fee, either a one-time payment or a monthly fee, the agents assigned to your family will educate and help you to either build a great credit score or teach you how to improve your score. Your credit score is more than a look at your use of credit. It also tells lenders what their repayment risks are if you were to obtain a loan from them. It signals to employers your ability to be trusted. It also lets insurance companies know the rates they are allowed to offer you on your auto insurance. Your total credit score consists of your repayment history (on time versus slow/late), the amount of credit you have versus the amount of credit you are using, and the type of credit you have (for instance revolving credit is less favorable than a mortgage).

Read Financial Books/Articles

Take the time to read books explaining some basic financial principles. This will help you to understand what you don't know, so you will know what subjects to seek help on. The following books will help you to develop basic financial literacy skills:

1. The Buffett Way - Robert G. Hagstrom
2. The Buffettology Workbook – Mary Buffett and David Clark
3. One Up on Wallstreet – Peter Lynch
4. Beating the Street- Peter Lynch
5. Cash Flow Quadrant – Robert Kiyosaki
6. Secrets of the Millionaire Mind – T. Harv Eker
7. Unshakeable – Tony Robbins
8. The Little Book that Beats the Market – Joel Greenblatt
9. The Richest Man in Babylon – George s. Clason

Other helpful resource are newsletters and articles written by those closest to the financial industry. Most of the top financial news can be found on the News section of Market

Watch, which can be downloaded as an app to your phone or other mobile device.

Set Your Priorities

Decide as a team what your family priorities are. If you take the time to focus on the important events that cost money, it is a lot easier to stay motivated when working together towards your goals. Once you know what your number-one priority is, you can set milestones (small steps) towards achieving your goal.

Using milestones lessens the pressure of trying to reach goals all at once. By setting small achievable steps, it will motivate you to continue on the journey by experiencing celebrations along the way. For instance, if you want to buy a new car, then setting aside $250/bi-monthly may be a short-term milestone in order to have a $10,000 down payment after a year and a half of saving. The same is true of wanting to get out of debt. You have to develop a plan, make adjustments along the way, check to see if you are on track, and create opportunities to increase income.

CHAPTER 7

WHY DOES THE STOCK MARKET SCARE YOU?

*"We were not taught financial literacy in school. It takes
a lot of work and time to change your thinking and to
become financially literate."* **– Robert Kiyosaki**

*"Wisdom is the principal thing; therefore, get wisdom: and
with all thy getting get understanding." Proverbs 4:7*

What's the problem? Why can't we trust financial advisors
to make sure we retire with enough money in the bank to
live well in retirement. It's because many financial advisors
don't have your best interest at heart, or at least, not ahead of
their own interest or that of their company's. This fact alone
should make you very afraid. What this means is, the advisor
can place you in investments where you may or may not see
growth in your portfolio, but they receive large and lucrative
commissions and fees. In other words, they get paid whether
you make money or not! How is this possible? Before he left
office, President Barack Obama's administration put forth a
ruling that would make financial advisors fiduciaries through

the Department of Labor, but that was squashed in 2018 by the Fifth Circuit Court (covers Texas, Louisiana, and Mississippi).

The fiduciary rule is officially dead. What its fate means to you!

Published: June 25, 2018 1:55 p.m. ET

By Alessandra Malito - Reporter

The controversial rule requiring advisers to act in their clients' best interests when it comes to managing retirement accounts is officially dead.

The Fifth Circuit Court, which covers Texas, Louisiana and Mississippi, confirmed this month that its split decision in March to end the Department of Labor's fiduciary rule has been finalized. It also ruled the DOL must pay for the costs of the appeal.

Why kill the rule? The court had concluded that the Department of Labor, which oversees the fiduciary rule, "overreached" with its mission. The fiduciary rule, also known officially as the "Conflict of Interest" rule, states advisers have to give conflict-free advice on retirement accounts, putting their clients' needs ahead of their own potential compensation. That means shifting away from commissions on various investment products and becoming completely transparent on what they do and the advice they provide.

The Obama administration, which proposed the rule, claimed it would save Americans $17 billion a year from conflicted advice. The U.S. rule was weaker than what other countries have in place to protect investors, such as in the U.K., where commissions are banned and advisers must pass harder tests, said Betsey Stevenson, a former member of the President's Council of Economic Advisers who worked on the fiduciary rule, and currently a public policy and economics professor at the University of Michigan. "With the court undoing that, it means you have to ask really hard questions if you're going to a financial adviser," she said.

Financial advisers saw this coming, especially after the Trump administration delayed the **rule's implementation**, and though some say they are disappointed by the turn of events, they seem hopeful that enough word has gotten out that *not all financial advice is good advice.* "The fact that it was so deeply fought on both sides has brought it to the forefront," said Jeffrey Levine, the chief executive and director of financial planning at BluePrint Wealth Alliance. Years ago, prospective clients never asked him if he was a fiduciary but today, the topic comes up with regularity. Though no one knows for sure what will become of the rule, it appears the concept of conflict-free advice is here to stay.

In its March decision, the Fifth Circuit Court said the rule defined financial advice and who gives it too broadly, and that it was "unreasonable." Opponents argue it will be too expensive to manage the accounts of small investors, and that it's possible for advisers to charge commissions without conflict.

Treasurers from 11 states have written to the SEC asking for a more stringent fiduciary rule, saying in a March 8 letter that "any standard less robust than [the DOL's rule] does not provide adequate protection for investors." Those states are Pennsylvania, Oregon, Iowa, Maryland, Rhode Island, Illinois, Washington, South Carolina, Vermont, Utah and Wyoming. "This implementation delay, and the accompanying non-enforcement agreement, represent a step back in terms of protecting the interests of retirement savers and investors," they wrote.

Small investors are at risk of being most affected by the overturning of the rule, as they may not be able to afford a financial planner or have enough saved to qualify for some advisers' services, and therefore go to anyone who could end up selling them unnecessary products, said McClanahan. She is warning investors to tread lightly when looking for a financial professional, and to urge legislators to find a common ground that would protect consumers and protect the consumer from "unscrupulous people who will take advantage of them." (Milto, 2018)

Even the states are afraid small investors (see above article) will be taken advantage of. It is extremely time consuming to properly and actively manage a portfolio. It means that an advisor has to be in tune with the financial markets daily/weekly/monthly, do research, make decisions, take actions, and do so for all their clients with portfolios designed specifically for each individual client. This is a monumental task. It screams the need for financial literacy at all levels of our society. Not everyone feels the same way. Some of the comments were troubling and I wanted to shed some light on them. Here are a few comments made by a few people on the above article:

Roe and Foxx Praise Circuit Court of Appeals Ruling to Vacate Obama-era Fiduciary Rule

WASHINGTON, March 16, 2018 | Lani Short (202-225-6356) | 1 comments

WASHINGTON – Rep. Virginia Foxx (R-NC), chairwoman of the House Committee on Education and the Workforce, and Rep. Phil Roe (R-TN), today issued the following statements after the Fifth Circuit Court of Appeals vacated the Obama-era fiduciary rule, a regulation that limited retirement savers' access to affordable financial advice and cost American families an estimated $17 billion a year.

"The fiduciary rule has been a disaster since day one, which is why I've fought to stop it since 2010," **Rep. Roe said.** *"Unfortunately, the Obama administration refused to listen to bipartisan warnings that the fiduciary rule could drive up the cost of financial advice for low- and middle-income families, and President Obama vetoed my legislation to stop the rule. I was glad when President Trump delayed implementing parts of the rule while the fight continued in the courts, but more needs to be done to ensure every American – no matter their background – has access to sound financial advice. The fiduciary rule was unquestionably a solution in search of a problem, which is exactly*

why this ruling is a victory for every American sav-ing toward retirement. I hope this will put an end to the misguided fiduciary rule once and for all, and that we can instead focus on how to improve protections for savers without potentially costing them access to advice."

"Millions of American families want to save for retirement, and the Obama Administration's fidu-ciary rule only made it harder for them to do so," **Chairwoman Foxx said.** *"We're glad the Fifth Circuit recognized this rule for the fundamentally flawed exercise in federal overreach that it truly was, and we will continue our work to make afford-able, sound retirement advice a reality for work-ers, families, and small businesses. H.R. 2823, the* Affordable Retirement Advice for Savers Act, *opens the door for low-and middle-income Amer-ican workers to access the solid retirement advice they want, and we're proud to offer this legislative solution for them." (Short, 2018)*

PugLady says: Replying to @DrPhilRoe @ USDOL
So, now they can push whatever financial fund makes the adviser more commissions? Hmmm. That doesn't seem right at all. Just another thing @ realDonaldTrump had his minions reverse because he wants to erase Obama's legacy.

Colby Preston says: Replying to @DrPhilRoe @ USDOL
It's a victory right up until your financial advisor sticks you in some terrible investment because

they get better fees/commissions and then your retirement disappears...but hey, everyone who has investments or retirement savings is a financial expert anyway right? So, no biggie...

You fail to realize the reason people pay a financial advisor in the first place. Not everyone has the time. That's why "they pay someone" else to help with those decisions...but don't let me stop you from thinking those people you're paying should have zero accountability.

Billy Big Bollocks *says: Replying to @BitoTx @ DrPhilRoe @USDOL*
Freedom of choice. No one is gonna hold your hand or stop you from making poor decisions

B-Town *says: Replying to @BitoTx @ johnyytsunami and 2 others*
If you can't manage relatively simple mutual funds or you have zero awareness of what your retirement advisor is doing then try reading a book or look up investing tactics online. Your retirement is your responsibility....

But they have enough time to cruise Facebook, Twitter etc. There's 24 hours in a day and retirement investing is far more important than many things in our life. Find time. Find good professionals if you hire for the job. It's not hard.

James Buman *@JamesBuman 17 Mar 2018*
Replying to @wally_six_0 @BitoTx and 3 others
Obviously people should find reputable professionals, but this does not mean that these prof. should not be held accountable when intentionally

screwing over their clients for gain. Your Dr. will be held accountable when intentionally killing you during a procedure, bad?

(Milto, 2018)

We are divided on the subject as you can read from the comments above. Some people believe having personal responsibility when it comes to high finance is the key. While others feel the government should do something to ensure the small investors are taken care of. Others feel that personal education and research is the key to financial awareness. Do you have the time to watch over your own investments? Should you be able to trust those to whom you give your money to for investment purposes? Lots of questions, but what is the answer? First, what are some other questions?

- Why have the Certified Financial Planners, Certified Financial Analysts, and Investment Advisors go through such extreme and extensive studies and tests, if you are not going to make them accountable for their decisions according to the prudent advisor policy?

- Why force the advisor to gain all this knowledge, just to say the people trusting them, need to read a book and then educate themselves, and become responsible for their own financial future?

- Why go through all the trouble of regulating any and everything with laws and rules of law, if the advisor doesn't have to be a fiduciary? Well, the question really is, whom does it benefit the most for the advisor not to be a fiduciary? Or, better yet, whom does it benefit if the advisor is a fiduciary?

You have every right to be afraid! Sometimes "fear" is healthy if it causes appropriate and corrective action!

Fearing the unknown and fearing the unfamiliar is natural. Most people fear change because change takes them out of their comfort zone. Any time we are uncomfortable, stress is introduced into our bodies. Stress puts undue pressure on your body and its organs. According to ActiveBeat.com:

Stress is a feeling most everyone is familiar with. While it may sometimes serve a helpful purpose, such as pushing us beyond preconceived physical and mental boundaries, it is most commonly associated with negative factors.

These include causes such as pressure or unhappiness at work, and other elements of life such as money, divorce, or the death of a loved one. If such stress can't be managed properly and persists on a long-term basis, it can lead to more serious health problems—including the following seven.

1. Heart problems such as increased risk of heart attacks and disease!

2. Obesity caused by the desire for carb-heavy foods which increase our feel good sensors with increased serotonin!

3. Diabetes is accelerated because of the increase in blood sugar levels in Type 1 and 2 diabetes with additional stress!

4. Depression is more prevalent due to the imbalances of neurotransmitter systems such as ser-

otonin, dopamine and norepinephrine due to chronic stress.

5. Gastrointestinal problems increase because stress activates the fight or flight response of the body and the body reacts by increasing levels of adrenaline!

6. Sleep deprivation and other related issues will increase due to increased levels of stress which in-turn cause more issues with sleep; a vicious cycle!

7. Dementia is possibly triggered with increased levels of stress because studies have shown stress causes the release a hormone known as cortisol, which "has been linked to problems with memory." And, as previously mentioned, there is a strong connection between stress and depression, a factor that has been linked to an increased risk of dementia. (Despres, 2019)

The question then becomes are you going to experience stress due to a lack of money, or because you have a lot of money? This book is written to help get rid of the stress associated with not having enough money in retirement and as you approach retirement. The information is only as good as you are willing to put the ideas and systems into practice. Since stress will occur throughout your life, make a decision to take at least one stressor out of the equation; the lack of money in retirement.

When we hear horror stories about people who lost millions in the stock market, we might have serious second thoughts about investing in stocks. With all the news coverage about people like Bernie Madoff and others it's hard to put your trust in a system that seems to be broken and sometimes manipulated. If you have never invested before nor had been taught how to invest, you may experience some "stress" concerning your money and how it is invested.

If you are afraid to put your money in the stock market, then you should not do so. But, on the other hand if you don't have any money left over at the end of the month and your bills outlast your paycheck, you may experience increase stress. Also, if you are like the majority of Americans you may not have enough money to retire to a comfortable lifestyle; which adds to your stress. If you can't retire on your savings and investments, you may experience more stress if you have to continue to work after normal retirement years.

What are your options? Some people put their money in annuities, others in mutual funds, some people only have savings accounts, and still others invest in real estate. There are still jobs in the government sector that offer pensions, and in the public service areas. The problem is still the same. Inflation, recessions, and trade wars can cause some, part, or most of your hard-earned savings/investments to disappear. When I was down to my last $7,000 in my 401K due to divorce and the aftermath of 9-11, I really didn't have a choice. I had to have a vehicle that was going to grow my investments faster than inflation and faster than a savings account, but without all the stress.

This is the reason I wrote this book. I wanted to help relieve stress when it came to investing. I wanted everyone who would educate themselves to understand, that with a few foundational investment strategies, anyone, and I do mean anyone, can become a millionaire. Armed with a systematic, dedicated, and consistent plan using either the stock market, mutual funds (may take a little longer), or using exchange traded funds an individual can gain riches. In the simplest terms, Exchange Traded Funds (ETFs) are funds that track indexes like the NASDAQ-100 Index, S&P 500, Dow Jones, etc. When you buy shares of an ETF, you are buying shares of a portfolio that tracks the yield and return of its native index. The main difference between ETFs and other types of index funds is that ETFs don't try to outperform their corresponding index, but simply replicate its performance. They don't try to beat the market; they try to be the market. (NASDQ. Com, 2019)

In Tony Robbins book "Unshakable" he discusses why he likes ETFs. He likes the simplicity of the low-risk, low fees, broad diversification, tax-efficient, and an investment that will mirror the market. You also have the option of adding bonds, REITs, and dividend-paying stocks to your overall portfolio that will help balance your overall investment strategy. He also states throughout the book that advisors who are not fiduciaries don't have to put the investor's interest ahead of their own. (Robbins, 2017)

Take a look at your investments. Ask your plan administrator at work to go over your retirement account with you at least once a year. If you have an advisor or a Certified Financial Planner (CFP) handling your money, you should strive to meet with them at a minimum of once a year, but twice a year is more ideal in order to make necessary adjustments to your portfolio.

The first question you should ask them is, "Are you a fiduciary?" If their answer is no, you should seek out an advisor that is a fiduciary. The reason for this is in the name. Fiduciary is a person or organization that acts on behalf of another person or persons to manage assets. Essentially, a fiduciary owes to that other entity the duties of good faith and trust. The highest legal duty of one party to another, being a fiduciary requires being bound ethically to act in the other's best interests.

A fiduciary might be responsible for general well-being, but often the task involves finances—managing the assets of another person, or of a group of people, for example. Money managers, financial advisors, bankers, accountants, executors, board members, and corporate officers all have fiduciary responsibility. A fiduciary's responsibilities or duties are both ethical and legal. When a party knowingly accepts the fiduciary duty on behalf of another party, they are required to act in the best interest of the principal, the party whose assets they are managing. This is what is known as a "prudent person standard of care," a standard that originally stems from an 1830 court ruling. (Kagan, 2019)

If you're like the majority of people, you probably need to step up your retirement- saving efforts. An October 2017 Government Accountability Office (GAO) analysis found that the median retirement savings for Americans between age 55 and 64 was $107,000. The GAO notes this sum would only translate into a $310 monthly payment if it was invested in an inflation-protected annuity.

Household savings in all retirement accounts have dramatically increased since their pre-recession levels including among Millennials ($9,000 in 2007 to $36,000 in 2017), Generation X ($32,000 to $71,000), and Baby Boomers ($75,000 to $157,000), according to a September 2018 report from the Transamerica Center for Retirement Studies. (Parker, 2019)

This ($310-600) doesn't sound like a whole lot of money to live on in your retirement years. If you are in your twenties and have some investments, take the time to read books on investments, or sit through an investment seminar, it will be worth the expense. It is critical that you know what is going on with your money, how much you have, where it is invested, and what your annual returns have been. If you are not up on this, you have to get comfortable asking questions, and educating yourself on all things financial.

Questions and suggestions for a Financial Advisor:

1. Are you a fiduciary?
2. How often can we review my portfolio?
3. What books do you suggest I read concerning financial literacy?
4. How will we choose the investments for my portfolio?
5. May I see your credentials for investment advice?
6. How much will you make in fees and commissions on my account?
7. What kind of research will you do before suggesting changes to my account?

Before choosing an advisor, make sure you go to FINRA's (Financial Industry Regulatory Authority) Broker Check (www.finra.org/brokercheck).

What Scares You?

Stock Market Crashes

- Markets move up and market move down, but it's when the moves are unexpected or severe that we label them as crashes. Since inception the market has had these so call "crashes" over twenty times. One thing they have in common is fear, and the fact that the markets always seem to recover. Of course, certain outdated/ outmoded sectors and businesses do not recover, but for the majority of listings on the exchanges, they survive and thrive after a large downturn.

- There have been about twenty-five significant drops and many more corrections. And yet, in the long-term, the market always goes up dramatically. As Buffett said, `the market started the century (1900) at 66. It ended it at 11,400. How did people lose money in such a period? They were trying to dance in and out of markets`.

- One of the reasons they were trying to dance in and out of markets is that they were petrified of these falls.

- They were trying to find the ideal time to `get in`, when market timing doesn't work.

- So, the average investor should just:
    - o   Invest through rain and shine
    - o   Not care if markets are up or down
    - o   Have a slight preference for falls unless they're within 5 years of retirement

    o Read investment books and older article to give you perspective. When you read about investors `terrified of markets going down to 400 from 600 in the early 60s` in a book, it sure gives you some perspective. In another 50 years people will think the same about people today who are terrified of markets falling. (Fayed, 2019)

What should you do when the market moves down? It seems everyone is happy when it moves up, but when it is down, sadness abounds. My educational enlightenment to you would be to buy as much stock as possible when it is on sale! Common people only have so much money to spend each month on investing. There is no better way to spend it when the market has a "so called" crash. In 2008, I stopped investing over a 10-month period from March through December and amassed approximately $35,000. In March of 2009, I purchased blue chip stocks that dropped over 45 percent in the preceding 12-month period. By, November of 2010 my portfolio had increased over 49 percent (the value of my portfolio dropped over 23 percent in 2008). Buying great companies on sale is a great strategy as touted by Warren Buffett and other contrarian investors. Contrarian is an investment style in which investors purposefully go against prevailing market trends by selling when others are buying, and buying when most investors are selling.

We have all heard the bad stories that surround investing, and what I have found in my research is many of these unfortunate events took place because a person invested, based on a hot tip," a new fad, or trying to get "rich quick."

Proper investing is not a get rich quick scheme! Investing properly requires the person managing the account/portfolio to have a well thought out process for selecting companies, evaluating companies, evaluating the current economic status, evaluating the future economy, and deciding when to purchase a security. Most importantly, if it's to be successful, the process has to be repeatable, not once, but over and over again!

Having an understanding of "Compound Interest" will lessen fear to zero! It's easy to duplicate and it happens automatically, over and over again (see Chapter 18–Financial Freedom). Once you understand how it works and realize that it's not rocket science, you will be able to relax and implement the process for continued growth over time.

Enron Scandal

- In 2001, the Enron scandal shook Wall Street to it very core, along with investor confidence. Enron was formed in 1985 following a merger between Houston Natural Gas Company and Omaha-based Inter-North Incorporated. Following the merger, Kenneth Lay, who had been the chief executive officer (CEO) of Houston Natural Gas, became Enron's CEO and chairman. Lay quickly rebranded Enron into an energy trader and supplier. Deregulation of the energy markets allowed companies to place bets on future prices, and Enron was poised to take advantage. In 1990, Lay created the Enron Finance Corporation and appointed Jeffrey Skilling, whose work as a McKinsey & Company consultant had impressed Lay, to head the new corporation....

- One of Skilling's early contributions was to transition Enron's accounting from a traditional historical cost accounting method to mark-to-market (MTM) accounting method, for which the company received official SEC approval in 1992. MTM is a measure of the fair value of accounts that can change over time, such as assets and liabilities. Mark-to-market aims to provide a realistic appraisal of an institution's or company's current financial situation, and it is a legitimate and widely used practice. However, in some cases, the method can be manipulated, since MTM is not based on "actual" cost but on "fair value," which is harder to pin down. Some believe MTM was the beginning of the end for Enron as it essentially permitted the organization to log estimated profits as actual profits.

- The market-to-market accounting approach was disastrous for Enron, because they got permission and formed SPVs (special purpose vehicles) in order to hide actual business losses that were not reported in the MTM accounting process. Their issue happened because using this method they built large assets such as a power plant, and immediately claim the projected profit on its books, even though the company had not made one dime from the asset. If the revenue from the power plant was less than the projected amount, instead of taking the loss, the company would then transfer the asset to an off-the-books corporation where the loss would go unreported.

- Eventually, the toxic SPVs carrying loads of debt, came to the attention of the SEC just prior to a merger with "Dynegy" fell through. Dynegy (NYSE: DYN), a company that had previously announced would merge with Enron, backed out of the deal on November28th. By December 2, 2001, Enron had filed for bankruptcy. The SEC took notice when Enron restated its earnings going back to 1997; Enron had losses of $591 million and had $628 million in debt by the end of 2000.

- Eventually Enron stock went into freefall and stopped at a price of $0.26.

- Enron paid out $21.7 billion to shareholders from 2004 – 2011. (Segal, 2019)

Madoff Madness

- If the 25 market drops don't scare you, and the Enron scandal doesn't make you flee, then the story of the biggest ponzi scheme in history should make you shiver!

- Bernard Lawrence "Bernie" Madoff is an American financier who executed the largest Ponzi scheme in history, defrauding thousands of investors out of tens of billions of dollars over the course of at least seventeen years, and possibly longer. He was also a pioneer in electronic trading and chairman of the Nasdaq in the early 1990s.

- Despite claiming to generate large, steady returns through an investing strategy called split-strike conversion, which is an actual trading strategy, Madoff simply deposited client funds into a single bank account that he used to pay existing clients who wanted to cash out. He funded redemptions by attracting new investors and their capital, but was unable to maintain the fraud when the market turned sharply lower in late 2008. He confessed to his sons—who worked at his firm but, he claims, were not aware of the scheme—on Dec. 10, 2008. They turned him in to the authorities the next day. The fund's last statements indicated it had $64.8 billion in client assets.

• The Ponzi scheme became a potent symbol of the culture of greed and dishonesty that, to critics, pervaded Wall Street in the run-up to the financial crisis. Madoff was sentenced to 150 years in prison and ordered to forfeit $170 million in assets, but no other prominent Wall Street figures faced legal ramifications in the wake of the crisis. (Keaton, 2019)

Financial Crisis of 2008

• Just when you thought it was safe to go back into the water, a giant shark came after you while you were sleeping in your home. Who knew sharks had legs? While you slept someone, or something took everything you hold dear and slammed it into the ground. Your pensions, you home value, your job, and in some cases your life. The financial crisis was more than a loss of jobs, decreasing home values, and total loss of investor confidence. It was about a loss of hope! America and the world had been sold a bill of fake goods that were not worth the paper on which they were printed! Since we all were on board, we all suffered (with the exception of the super-rich). I get it, everyone wanted a home, everyone wanted low interest rates, and everyone wanted to make money by any means necessary. The problem was the methods used to defraud and scheme, and hide were so new and innovative, the very people that helped cause the crisis, were asked to help lead the charge to fix the problem.

- The 2008 financial crisis was the worst economic disaster since the Great Depression of 1929. It occurred despite Federal Reserve and Treasury Department efforts to prevent it.

- It led to the Great Recession. That's when housing prices fell 31.8 percent, more than the price plunge during the Depression. Two years after the recession ended, unemployment was still above 9 percent. That's not counting discouraged workers who had given up looking for work.

- But why did it happen in the first place. In short, greed! This seems to be a re-occurring theme. When someone with power, position, and privilege, feel entitled to more, bad things happen to those less fortunate. The first sign that the economy was in trouble occurred in 2006. That's when housing prices started to fall. At first, realtors applauded. They thought the overheated housing market would return to a more sustainable level.

- Realtors didn't realize there were too many homeowners with questionable credit. Banks had allowed people to take out loans for 100 percent or more of the value of their new homes. Many blamed the Community Reinvestment Act. It pushed banks to make investments in subprime areas, but that wasn't the underlying cause.

- The Gramm-Rudman Act was the real villain. It allowed banks to engage in trading profitable derivatives that they sold to investors. These mortgage-backed securities needed home loans as collateral. The derivatives created an insatiable demand for more and more mortgages. Greed!

- Hedge funds and other financial institutions around the world owned the mortgage-backed securities. The securities were also in mutual funds, corporate assets, and pension funds. The banks had chopped up the original mortgages and resold them in tranches. That made the derivatives impossible to price. Greed!

- The first signs of the financial crisis appeared in 2007. Banks panicked when they realized they would have to absorb the losses. They stopped lending to each other. They didn't want other banks giving them worthless mortgages as collateral. No one wanted to get stuck holding the bag. As a result, interbank borrowing costs, called Libor, rose. This mistrust within the banking community was the primary cause of the 2008 financial crisis.

- A group of bankers, financiers, law-makers, and other sorts got together and offered up Bear-Sterns Bank as the sacrificial lamb to the slaughter. It was the name associated with the initial crisis, but that was not the end. On September 17, 2008, the crisis created a run on money market funds. Companies park excess cash there to earn interest on it overnight. Banks then use those funds to make short-term loans. During the run, companies moved a record $144.5 billion out of their money market accounts into even safer Treasury bonds. If these accounts had gone bankrupt, business activities and the economy would have ground to a halt.

- That crisis called for a massive government intervention. Three days later, Treasury Secretary Henry

Paulson and Fed Chair Ben Bernanke submitted a $700 billion bailout package to Congress. Their fast response stopped the run. But Republicans blocked the bill for two weeks. They didn't want to bail out banks. They only approved the bill after global stock markets almost collapsed.

- The $700 billion bailout package had some issues, so newly elected President Barack Obama didn't use the remaining money allocated for TARP. He didn't want to bail out any more businesses. Instead, he asked Congress for an economic stimulus package. On February 17, 2009, he signed the American Recovery and Reinvestment Act. It had tax cuts, stimulus checks, and public works spending. By 2011, it put $831 billion directly into the pockets of consumers and small businesses. It was enough to end the financial crisis by July 2009. (Amadeo, 2019)

It's Everywhere

A lot of people and companies have put in a lot of effort to keep the investing public safe from harm. The biggest danger is the investor themselves. This means that the lack of financial literacy led to the crisis discussed above. Because we depend on so-called experts, we are susceptible to TV pundits, the too-good-to be true "hot tips," and many other get-rich quick schemes. Becoming financially free is more of a marathon journey of time and not a sprint. It is important to have a fiduciary advisor to take the journey with you, because they will keep you from the known pit-falls.

The fiduciary rule is about more than adviser pay. Here's why that matters.

Published: Aug 16, 2017 9:17 a.m. ET

Advisers who can't meet the standard might face legal jeopardy.

Most of the discussion over the Labor Department's fiduciary rule, which took effect in June, has centered around the "duty of loyalty," which requires financial advisers to put their clients' best interest ahead of their own compensation.

But that, according to Michael Kitces — a prominent expert on financial advice and publisher of the Nerd's Eye View blog — has come at the expense of a focus on the fiduciary's "duty of care," an oversight that could expose financial services' companies that don't sufficiently train their people, or hire skilled practitioners, to legal jeopardy.

The duty of care, in short, is concerned with fiduciary advisers' competence and commitment to thoughtful advice.

Read: Forget the fiduciary standard — financial advisers need a code of ethics

"What the duty of care essentially requires is that fiduciaries only give advice after conducting the appropriate due diligence, that they make sure they have a process to make decisions in a prudent manner," Kitces said in a video played at the Retirement Income Industry Association conference at Salem State University. "This means you really have to have a clear process for conducting that due diligence and making the decisions — and, more important, that the advisers have the expertise to be able to arrive at a prudent decision after going through that process."

That, Kitces said, "Is a pretty big deal."

Why? Because, he said, too many financial advisers can't meet that standard. "The reality is still that financial advisers can hold (themselves) out as financial advisers or retirement experts to the public with really nothing more than a high school diploma and passing a two to three-hour regulatory exam," he said. "And the high school diploma is optional."

Read: The best way for retirement-plan sponsors to hire a fiduciary

That, according to Kitces, means that many so-called advisers may try to meet the duty of loyalty but have little to no chance of meeting the duty of care because they lack the training and expertise. And that could lead to big class-action lawsuits against major financial institutions, according to Kitces.

Some attorney is going to come along and say, 'So, explain to me how your thousands of retirement advisers would possibly know how to give 'best interest advice' to their retiree clients when only a fraction of them even have the training and education of a formal retirement designation program,' he said. "It's going to be a very awkward conversation for that company's legal department."

Republicans in Congress and the Trump administration's Labor Department are fighting to relax the rule. "But at some point, the focus will shift from fighting about the rules to paying attention to how they are being enforced," Kitces said. "And when it does, I think you are going to see a new wave of scrutiny on who says they give 'best interest' retirement advice and who is a retirement expert."

Jeffrey Levine, the CEO and director of financial planning at BluePrint Wealth Alliance, agreed that advisers who deliver retirement advice under the Labor Department's fiduciary rule will need advanced training.

"There has to be more than just passing the series 6 or 7 or 66," he said, referring to the licenses for financial advisers. "It's been an industry problem for a long time, but now it may catch up to advisers in a more powerful way. Passing those tests are a minimum, baseline requirement. But to really act in someone's best interest, you need more."

Read: Why more financial advisers may become like Costco — subscription-based.

What sort of training might that be? Levine speculated that industry bodies, academic institutions, or financial services' firms could offer advanced programs, rigorous self-study curricula or advanced degrees and designations, suggesting that they include a method for staying current as laws, strategies and products evolve. In the blog referenced above, Kitces noted at least two designations that meet the sort of training he thinks is required.

"Advisers can further protect themselves and their clients by working with their other service providers to make sure they're being comprehensive," Levine said.

"Don't be afraid to call for reinforcements," he said. "Part of meeting the duty of care is making sure you are only advising on matters to which you can provide competent advice. If you're not big into taxes, reach out to the client's tax preparer to make sure your proposed move doesn't trigger any unforeseen consequences."

The same goes for other areas, such as estate planning and asset protection. "There's nothing wrong with a team approach," he said. "It doesn't lower the adviser's credibility...If anything, it can help assure a client that when the adviser really is delivering advice, they are doing so with confidence."

The fiduciary rule, as it exists today, requires that advisers do more than the minimum in terms of getting to know their customer, according to Levine. "That means learning about their goals, objectives, concerns and family situations," he said.

"The old adage 'know your client' needs to become 'really know your client,' Levine said. "To truly act in someone's best interest, you need to know more than some cursory info, such as their age, their risk tolerance, their income and asset levels."

The fiduciary rule requires that advisers not just provide advice but monitor and revise that advice as needed. "Life happens and when it does, changes often need to be made," Levine said. "Ongoing monitoring of clients' lives should be stepped up."

Lastly, Levine suggested advisers must not provide retirement advice in a vacuum. Instead, they need to become skilled at offering comprehensive advice, because doing less could mean they aren't fulfilling the duty of care.

"At the end of the day, I think the duty of care is best served when a client is making decisions based on a complete financial plan," Levine said.

This story was first published on August 2, 2017. Robert Powell is editor of Retirement Weekly, *published by MarketWatch.*

CHAPTER 8

OVERCOMING YOUR FEARS

"Becoming successful financially, whether in business or career, is not about becoming somebody else, but learning how to be yourself." – Henry Ong (Ong, 2014)

"Arise; for this matter belongeth unto thee: we also will be with thee: be of good courage, and do it." Ezra 10:4

How do you get over the fear of the stock market? My initial answer is, education, but the real answer varies depending on who you ask. Although some people run from the market, others have done quite well. Some people do well in spite of all the bad news, turmoil of the financial industry, and the ups and downs of the stock market. What is their secret? One person that was uneducated in the matters of investing, but over a period time became very wealthy, was Theodore Johnson. Johnson, a UPS worker who never earned more than $14,000 a year, always used 20 percent of his pay to purchase company stock. He also put every yearly bonus into company stock. By age 90 he had accumulated $70 million. The education here is to recognize the power of disciplined savings and long-term compound interest! (Robbins, 2017)

When Johnson retired in 1952, he had amassed $700,000 and had worked with UPS for 28 years. By using reverse calculations, I was able to calculate compound average growth rate (CAGR). In order to grow from $700K to $70 million he had to average 11.89 percent compound interest a year for 39 years in retirement assuming he did not contribute any additional funds into his account. Just to clarify the differences, the median income per family was $3300 a year in 1952, which makes Mr. Johnson's salary approximately $123K in today's dollars. With that being said, he could afford to save 20 percent of his salary and still have enough to live well above the median income of the rest of the country. To most of us this seems an impossibility, but with the proper education, putting 20 percent aside will not be too difficult (keep reading).

The time value of money works on one premise and that is "seed, time, and harvest! If you plant a seed from an ear of corn, give it time to grow; then it would be reasonable to expect a harvest of corn when the seed matures.

Not investing (major vehicle to gain wealth over time) is like a farmer who has seed to plant, but is afraid of the weeds, the lack of rain, the animals, or disease that may harm his crop. Instead of planting the seed, he decides to eat the seed, to make bread from the seed, or to give the seed away. During the time of harvest, the farmer will not have anything to show for his efforts.

Over the past ten years the broad markets have been consistent over time. We know they go up and down but over the run from July 2009 to July 2019, they have all returned greater than a 10 percent CAGR. The DOW returned a CAGR of 12.0 percent, the NSADQ 16.46 percent, and the S&P 500 returned 12.85 percent over the same period.

According to Tony Robbins, in his book "Unshakable,"

you get real and honest with yourself and realized that unless you have some secret sauce, unequaled analytical skills or superior information there is no reason on earth that you should believe you can outperform the market. He suggests that you purchase a portfolio of low-cost index funds (most cost an average of .50 percent/year) and invest in them over the long haul, no matter what the market is doing. By doing this you will be able to receive at least the overall market returns. In other words, you will grow and add value as the companies represented in the broad markets grow and do well. The costs are low, and you will be as diversified as possible. (Robbins, 2017) In a quote he goes on to say, "By admitting to yourself that you have no special advantage, you give yourself an enormous advantage!"

Education Is The Real Key To Success.

In order to feel comfortable with buying stocks and or index funds, you will have to understand the basics of purchasing stocks and other securities. You will have to read several books and articles (see references appendix section) to know just how simple it is to allow your money to work for you. You have to be open to learning basic investment terms and procedures, rules and some regulations regarding the stock market. Even if you decide to only purchase mutual funds or index funds as suggested by Tony Robbins, at least you will feel comfortable in doing so and you will know what questions to ask anyone you allow to handle your money. Although I don't have any special sauce as quoted by Tony Robbins, what I do have is a desire to help others realize that the best way to invest is to select stocks from companies that you already purchase goods or services from. So, maybe my desire to help others could be considered my special sauce.

I began sharing and educating others with what I experienced with the financial industry in 2012. From 2006 through 2012, I was on a journey. I talked and shared with anyone who would listen. I understood how poorly our citizens were educated on finances. Most of the laws and rules around finance were written and created by the rich and powerful, either those in congress or financial institutions or lobbyists. These awesome methods of achieving wealth and power never made it down to the masses of society or to the classrooms. Thereby leaving a huge educational gap across a large swath of Americans. I also found the lack of education extended from people with low incomes to high, blue collar workers to those in corporate America, and across all ethnic and racial backgrounds.

Not only did I find a lack of education, but for the most part, with the exception of a few people, there was a sense of apathy concerning finances. This was especially true for those earning greater than $200K per year. Many people with these large incomes became vulnerable to the desire to ensure their money would be available for retirement, but due to little or no financial literacy they gave into the scare tactics and the volatile nature of the overall markets.

Get Your Advice From Proven Fiduciary Experts.

Getting your advice from television, friends, hot tips, and other anecdotal sources can cause problems with your account. It caused a friend of mine to put $200,000 into Ford stock, and as soon as it went up a few cents, he would sell it all. A few days later he would buy it again due to something he heard on television but sell it because of what he read in a newspaper article. After two years, he only had $250,000, that was due to what his company had added to his 401K. His net gain/loss was zero percent. His problem was he did not have a system or a process to follow. He blindly put his money into the next best thing as it was suggested by friends, TV, news reports, etc. It wasn't until he read a few suggested books and talked to me that his account settled down and started a greater than 20 percent year over year growth. At the writing of this book, four years later, his account is just shy of $1 million. He is still in his forties and has at least 20 working years remaining to continue to use this process to grow his nest egg.

There are many experts and advisors who will charge you one-half and up to 3 percent of your total portfolio, in order to help you with investment and retirement decisions.

Take Baby Steps

Start slow and don't be in a hurry to get rich overnight. If you take your time to learn as you go, you will be well ahead of the game! Read and ask questions of financial educators and advisors when they are speaking or giving seminars. Fill-up a small library with financial books to take with you to read and take notes. Follow a Plan.

CHAPTER 9

RESET YOUR MINDSET

Although I graduated with honors from Regis University with an MBA in Finance and Accounting, I was no closer to finding out how to really decide if the stock market was really for me. The financial crisis was just beginning its downward spiral, and most people felt helpless while the powers at the top of the financial food chain were licking their chops. Whenever there is a negative market condition, recession, or a big downturn in the economy, wealth changes hands. The historic flow is typically from the middle and lower class towards those with more resources and financial literacy!

My college professors had all worked either in banking or in a regulatory capacity, so they knew the basics of investing, but none the secrets of investing! Because so much was missing from the picture, I was drawn to read about the men and women who had gained success trading stocks. The following are a short list of books I recommend to anybody who wants to take control of their financial future.

"Warren Buffett Way"

I absolutely loved reading about the "Oracle of Omaha"

and his childhood. He did not lead a boring life, and his story kept me engaged from start to finish. It chronicles his life from early childhood, to starting a few businesses as a young man, to campaigning for his father running for public office, to meeting the rich and powerful in Washington, DC, and finally how he began on his journey to becoming rich over time.

"Richest Man in Babylon"

This book gives a biblical as well as a practical view of money and wealth. It chronicles the basic premise of smart investing through the eyes of a man who was like you and me. He wasn't special in any particular way, but he had saved money and was looking for ways to put his money to work. Initially, he made several mistakes before finally realizing he had to stick with the investments he was familiar with.

This book is one of my favorites. I first read this book when I was a teenager. I read it again upon my matriculation from Regis. It was still fascinating that the principles I learned in my youth, still applied after earning an MBA.

This book is definitely a page turner and the best part is its biblically based and timeless!

"Beating the Street"

My initial introduction into the world of investing led me to a mutual fund called Fidelity Magellan. At the time it was run but none other than Peter Lynch. This book taught me how to build a great stock portfolio using what I already knew and by combining that with a little research, you can realize great returns on your portfolio like many of the so-called experts. His insight also helped me recognize game changers through the charting of patterns not only in the stock prices, but in the way the world around us was changing. He expressed his method for picking companies for the fund included what he learned from his wife, children, neighbors, and other indicators that led to his success.

"Unshakeable"

I loved reading Unshakeable. I felt a kindred spirit in Tony Robins because we both recognize the deficiency of financial literacy in our country and the world. His observations and comments were all near and dear to my heart because I talk to everyday people with everyday problems; I feel the pain and anguish of not knowing what you don't know. The financial industry as a whole has some serious work to do to police itself and this book clearly lays out this fact. This is especially true when it comes to mutual funds and financial planners. The problem is the very people who are supposed to watch and help your money grow don't always have your best interest at heart. Unfortunately, when a planner has many clients and not enough time to devote to each individual person, the fund is supposed to do the work. But as Tony points out, the fund is set up to make the institution money and profits, whether the fund itself produces adequate increased returns for the client.

The fees being charged by the mutual funds sometimes cripple many accounts before they get out of the starting gate. Tony is convinced that the best way for the individual investor to get started is through the use of Exchange Traded Funds (ETFs). He lays out his premise for this type of investing citing its simplicity, low fees, and the ability to do as well as the overall market over time. It takes time to get rich, so don't be in a hurry.

CHAPTER 10

WHAT ON EARTH IS A DARK POOL?

"Orders in dark pools are like ice bergs. For a trade to take place, a resting bid, or buyer, has to be present when a seller initiates a sale. Many times both sides are not present at the same moment as orders are cancelled and replaced, these orders are referred to as 'ships passing in the night.'" **– D. Keith Ross, Chief Executive Officer of PDQ Enterprises**

"Therefore, whatsoever ye have spoken in darkness shall be heard in the light;" **Luke 12:3**

Although it sounds scary, it's not. The name is a simple reflection of the lack of transparency for the activities that happen in the dark pool.

"Dark pools are an ominous-sounding term for private exchanges or forums for securities trading. However, unlike stock exchanges, dark pools are not accessible by the investing public. Also known as "dark pools of liquidity," these exchanges are so named for their complete lack of transparency. Dark pools came about primarily to facilitate block trading by institutional investors who did not wish to impact the markets with their large orders and obtain adverse prices for their trades.

Dark pools were cast in an unfavorable light in Michael Lewis' bestseller *Flash Boys: A Wall Street Revolt,* but the reality is that they do serve a purpose. However, their lack of transparency makes them vulnerable to potential conflicts of interest by their owners and predatory trading practices by some high-frequency traders. (Percardo, 2019)

The first time I noticed something weird happening in the stock market that didn't seem to have a plausible explanation was when Apple (AAPL) stock dropped from ~$132 to around $90/share over a period of a few months. Television analyst were disagreeing with each other as to the cause. Some were saying it was because of the competition from Samsung, and others were blaming slow iWatch sales. In the end it appears to have been a dark pool event.

In mid-2015, a billionaire investor sold over ~7 million shares of AAPL. This excess number of shares were not sold openly, but in the dark pool and eventually affected the secondary market. The sale of these securities was not revealed until the beginning of December. After a bit of investigation, I stumbled on an article explaining an area on the web that allows institutional investors, billionaires, hedge funds, and others with large transactions to conduct business with each other, so as to not negatively affect the overall market. Intrigued as I was, I was still thinking how unfair a place like this actually existed, where the ultra-rich get to trade with each other. Later, I realized that unless a platform like this existed, our stock market (prices) would be more volatile.

The Bottom Line

Dark pools provide pricing and cost advantages to buy-side institutions such as mutual funds and pension funds, which hold that these benefits ultimately accrue to the retail investors who own these funds. However, dark pools' lack of transparency makes them susceptible to conflicts of interest by their owners and predatory high frequency trade (HFT) firms. HFT controversy has drawn increasing regulatory attention to dark pools, and implementation of the proposed "trade-at" rule could pose a threat to their long-term viability. (Percardo, 2019)

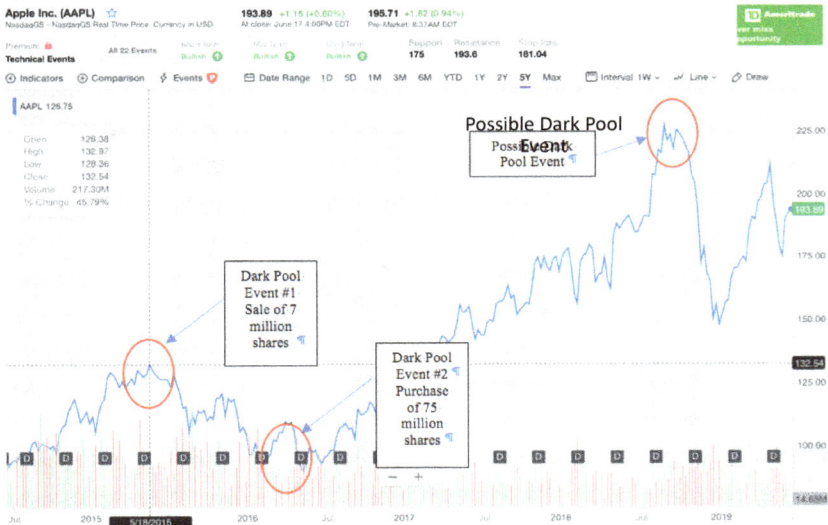

(Apple, 2019)

There are several you tube videos that go into detail about dark pools and how they work. If you follow a simple technique, taught in detail in a later Chapter, "When to Buy," you will be able to profit greatly when large transactions from the dark pool affect the overall market.

In the spring of 2016, the downward trend of AAPL's stock price reversed and began a meteoric climb to over $225/share by the summer of 2018. (See chart above) That was a hundred percent increase in less than three years if you took advantage of a great company's stock being sold at a great discount. The dark pool cannot be blamed for all volatile transactions, but once you understand that these events exist you will be better prepared when these events do occur. You will be able to purchase the stock of solid, household name, game changing companies at a deep discount. This is not considered "timing the market," but a strategy as to when to enter a volatile market. If I was in the market for a car, I would much rather purchase the car on sale for 30-40 percent off, rather than paying full price, or worst yet, paying a premium. When a large sale happens in the dark pool, eventually the residue from that large sale will drive the price of a stock down. The same is true of a large purchase in the dark pool. The whole idea of this area where these transactions are being held, is to not to negatively/positively affect the market causing panic selling or buying in the secondary market. Once it is disclosed that these large transactions have taken place, the secondary market reacts regardless of the 4-6 week delay of disclosure to the public. Let's face it, we would like to "channel" Warren Buffet actions in the market if we could, so we do the next best thing, we buy/sale what he buys and sales.

The biggest problem with the dark pool is during the time immediately following a massive transaction, and there is no rhyme or reason as to why a particular stock price is rising or falling.

Because it is known to only a few players, the pundits on television go back and forth as to the rise and decline of the price of a stock, adding to the volatility of the market. I try to explain that all the dark pool does, is create wonderful opportunities for investors wanting to purchase a stock (dark pool sale) or a selling opportunity for those wanting to sell at a nice profit (dark pool purchase). How can you, the Common Millionaire, tell if it's a dark pool event?

AAPL Apple Inc.
222.11 +7.66 222.43 +0.32
At Close   After Hours

1M   3M   6M   1Y   2Y   5Y   **10Y**

Open	220.42	Vol	34.97M	52W H
High	222.88	P/E	20.12	52W L
Low	216.84	Mkt Cap	1.073T	Avg Vo

This rise in stock price was due partially to that dark pool event when Warren Buffett purchased 75 million shares of AAPL in the Spring of 2016.

What Should You Do?

Looking at the above chart, try to imagine the slope of the overall curve of the price of Apple stock. Although the price moves up and down the overall trend for a company like Apple, a game-changer, is up. For the long-term investor, a purchase along this curve at any time for the past nine years would have resulted in an overall gain if held until September of 2018. At that time AAPL hit an all-time intra-day high of ~$228.87/share, but just a few months later the stock price was in free-fall to an intra-day low of ~$146.59/share in mid-December. If you worry about what is being said on the news reports as to what's going on with Apple, you may get confusing and often contradictory information. Don't let that sway you but be determined to purchase the shares in spite of the price decrease (go against your own emotion), and later you will reap the benefits of a great company going on sale!

- <u>Note:</u> Visit www.youtube.com to watch Dark Pool videos for more information on this topic.

CHAPTER 11

WHAT TO BUY?

"Financial literacy is not an end in itself, but a step-by-step process. It begins in childhood and continues throughout a person's life all the way to retirement. Instilling the financial-literacy message in children is especially important, because they will carry it for the rest of their lives. The results of the survey are very encouraging, and we want to do our part to make sure all children develop and strengthen their financial-literacy skills."
– **George Carl, chairman of the National CPA Financial Literacy Commission**

"Who, when he had found one pearl of great price, went and sold all that he had, and bought it." Matthew 13:46

What Products And Services Do You Use?

Have you ever heard of these: Apple, Netflix, Facebook, Visa, Boeing, Salesforce, or Amazon?

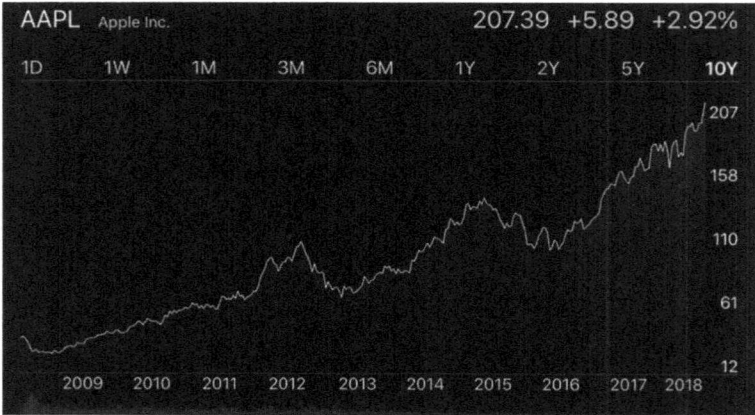

Apple grew 3500% over the ten-year period from 2008 through 2018.

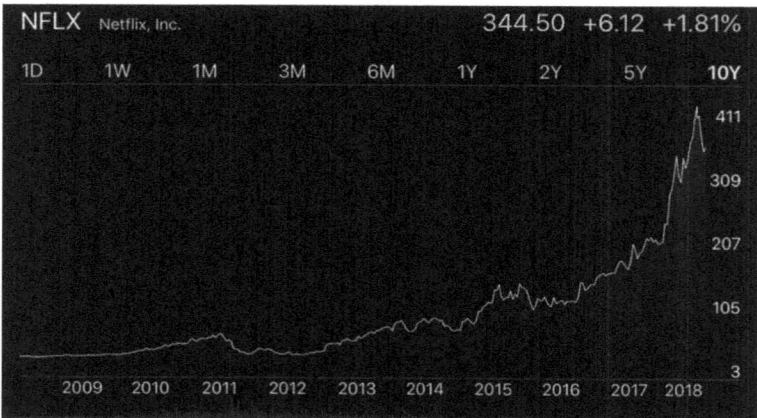

Netflix grew a whopping 12,500% from 2008 through 2018.

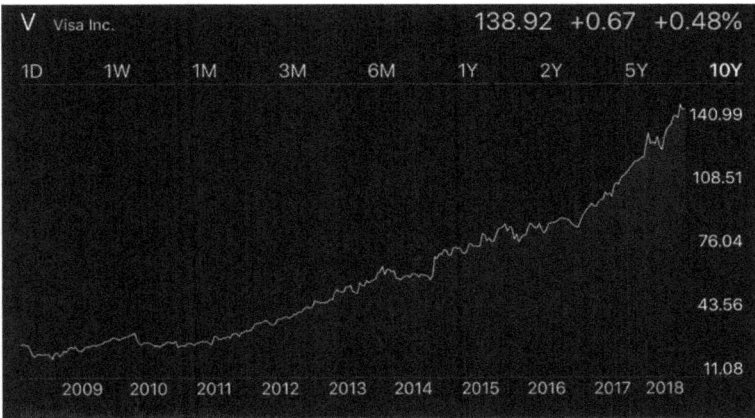

Over that same period, Visa grew by over 1300%.

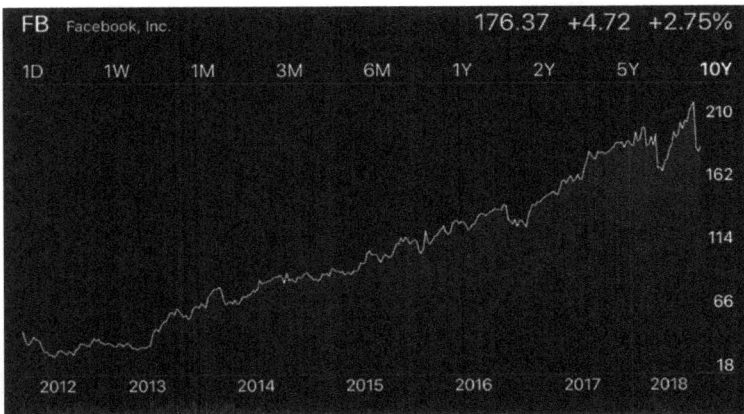

Facebook also saw an increase of 2000%.

What About The Children

I am often asked, "When is the best time to start investing?" My short answer is at "birth." The sooner the better is my motto. As soon as you can start generating compound interest the sooner you will achieve financial freedom. Of course, a baby is not capable of opening an account or conducting business, but parents and grandparents should do it on their behalf.

For our first grandson (now 3 years old) we put aside $50.00 per month, along with his other grandparents and both parents. During some months like December and his birthday month, he may average $400-500, that will be added to his account. If we apply the time value of money to his account and put his money to work in the stock market of goods and services, his mother and father use on his behalf we get the following:

Average monthly contribution: $250 ($50 per month per parent and grandparent)

Average annual interest rate: 15% (based on a balanced portfolio of great companies)

Number of years until 18 years old: 15

Number of years until 30 years old: 27

Amount saved to date in account: $10,000.00

Total amount available at 18 years old (does not include taxes withheld): $260,690.03

Total amount available at 30 years old (does not include taxes withheld): $1,577,833.27

Although taxes will have to be paid on the money there are strategies that help mitigate the amount of tax that will have to be paid (different book). Using the EZ-Calculators the following should be entered into the following areas; Present Value (PV), Payment (PMT), Rate, Periods (Number of months), then click on the Future Value (FV) in order to calculate the money available at 18 years old and 30 years old. Sure, there may be months that investment will go down as we see all year, but the beauty of it is they all tend to rebound, especially the great companies! (See calculations below)

‹ Home	**TVM Calculator** Advanced ?	
Present Value	**-10,000**	**PV**
Payment	**-250**	**PMT**
Future Value	**260,690.03**	**FV**
Annual Rate%	**15**	**Rate**
Periods	**180**	**Periods**
Compounding		**Monthly**
Mode	**End**	Beginning
Decimal	**Two** Three Four	Five
Instruction	**Reset**	**Email**

Note: Enter the known values and click the Button on the right to calculate the corresponding unknown value.

Calculations from 3 to 18 years old.

Remember to use a negative sign for the PV and the PMT because money is going into the account and not being taken out. This chart shows the results of using a consistent strategy over a period of time in order to grow his money. Some of the money could be protected from taxes if placed in a 529 Plan (college savings plan) with a participating state. New York, Ohio, Utah, West Virginia, Georgia, and South Carolina are ranked amongst the states with the best rated plans. Still some of the money can be protected if placed in a custodial account, a Coverdell education account, your Roth IRA account, and/or use a trust fund. The immediate goal is to begin savings for your children as soon as they are born, putting aside what you can each month with the help of other income producing adults in the child's life.

‹ Home	**TVM Calculator** Advanced ?
Present Value **-10,000**	**PV**
Payment **-250**	**PMT**
Future Value **1,577,833.27**	**FV**
Annual Rate% **15**	**Rate**
Periods **320**	**Periods**

Compounding   **Monthly**

Mode	End	Beginning

Decimal	Two	Three	Four	Five

Instruction	**Reset**	**Email**

Note: Enter the known values and click the Button on the right to calculate the corresponding unknown value.

Calculations from 3 to 30 years old.

Remember the key to successful investing is consistent, persistent, and intentional investing over time, understanding what to buy and when without being fearful of the ups and downs. If the children are taught how, when, and the whys of investing, they will be able to continue this trend and pass it down to their children and grandchildren as well. Why doesn't this happen? Fear, lack of financial education, apparent lack of funds, apathy, and a sense of entitlement.

Keeping Up With The Joneses

Some of the best advice I ever received was STOP trying to keep up with the Jones'. Tying your feeling of self-worth to what other people show and demonstrate may lead to poor financial decision making. This phenomenon starts at a very young age when in a child's mind every toy and exciting thing should be theirs and these little tykes will try to take it or will cry until they get it. Unfortunately, this trait can continue into adulthood unless it is taught out of us or trained out of us. If you try to impress people that don't really care about you by going into debt to buy the biggest and the best life has to offer, many times you will find yourself in serious debt and living paycheck to paycheck. How does a million-aire look anyway! Most millionaires don't look and act like millionaires. According to Drs. Thomas Stanley and William Danko, in their New York Times best-seller, The Millionaire Next Door, they describe the American millionaire quite differently than imagined. How would they describe themselves?

1. Males in their mid-late 50s, married with 3 children.

2. The number-one income producer in the family.

3. Either self-employed (20 percent), retired, or work in dull businesses such as welders, contractors, farmers, pest controllers, owners of mobile home parks.

4. Fifty-percent of our wives do not work outside of the home.

5. Have a combined household income (taxable

income) of approximately $131,000 a year.

6. Saves/invests 20 percent of income in a combination of emergency funds, investment funds, and savings.

7. Homeowner with homes valued at an average of $320,000.

8. Have an average net worth of $1.6 million.

9. Eight percent did not receive an inheritance, but are first-generation affluent.

10. Live well below our means.

11. Drive used American cars.

12. Married to women that are meticulous planners and budgeters.

13. Fairly well-educated, 4 in 5 are college graduates.

14. We spend heavily on education for our children and grandchildren.

15. Two-thirds of us work between 45-55 hours per week.

(Stanley & Danko, 1996)

The typical millionaire is a hard-working man or woman that lives below their means, who is a homeowner, believes in education, and consistently invests in things that they are familiar with.

Game Changers

The biggest discovery I made during my journey from the

financial ashes of my life was the fact that there were stocks that grew over 1000 percent over a period of ten years. It wasn't the fact they existed that surprised me, but the way I discovered it. My wife and I were looking for a place to share a meal after a long day at church. It was late Sunday night around nine-thirty and the restaurants near our home would not seat us for dinner after nine-thirty. After two unsuccessful attempts to get seated, my wife suggested Popeye's chicken. Upon arriving at Popeye's, we decided to go in to order because the drive-through line was very long (down the block and around the corner). When we drove to the front of the building, we saw that the lines inside were no better (three lines and ten people deep). Instead we went home and immediately I opened the computer and searched for the ticker symbol for Popeye's Chicken (Popeye's is no longer traded publicly). What I found astonished me in that after doing the calculations, I realized that a company as common a Popeye's, which a lot of common people eat there, was doing really well as an investment. Here's the chart I found:

November 2008 close price - $4.03

After I did the math that night in November 2013, I realized that something so familiar and close to me was able to return a profit of over 1000 percent after only a few years had to be special. But I was not convinced, so I began digging to find others.

November 2013 close price - $43.59

Doing the math revealed the following:

Beginning Price: $4.03 (November 2008)

Ending Price: $43.59 (November 2013)

Total Time elapsed: 5 Years

Compounded Annual Return on Investment: 61%

Overall Return on Investment: 981.64%

Simple Annualized ROI: 196.33%

Return on Investment (ROI) Calculator

| Amount Invested | $4.03 |
| Amount Returned | $43.59 |

Investment Time:
○ Use Dates   ○ Use Length

From Nov ▾ 7 ▾ 2008
To   Nov ▾ 7 ▾ 2013

Calculate

Result	
Investment Gain	$39.56
ROI	981.64%
Annualized ROI	61.00%
Investment Length	5.00 years

■ Invested 91%
■ Profit 9%

This revelation was a game changer for me because the next day, I purchased 250 shares and watched it grow over the next four years to $79.00 (the company was sold in 2017 and the stock is no longer publicly traded). Over that time, I ended up with over 500 shares of Popeyes' stock and realized an overall compounded return of around 20 percent per year. Although my average return was not as high as the historical average, I still was doing better than I was ever told was possible by financial planners and mutual fund managers.

So, I intentionally sought out other companies that could potentially have a 1000 percent return over a ten year period. What I found were companies like Apple (AAPL), Netflix (NFLX), Visa (V), Starbucks (SBUX), Nike (NKE), McDonalds (MCD), Amazon (AMZN), Boeing Aerospace (BA), Microsoft (MSFT), Mastercard (MA), AutoZone (AUTO), Facebook (FB), Lockheed Martin (LMT), Chipotle (CMG), Green Mountain Coffee Roasters (GMCR), Vail Mountain Resorts (MTN), and Home Depot (HD). But what do all these companies have in common? They are all game changers!

If we look at each of them closely, we see that they each played a role in shaping our future:

AAPL – Changed forever the concept of what a cell phone can do, and the endless uses for powerful handheld devices such as laptops and iPads. As I travel the world, it is the most used and recognized brand of mobile devices in the world (with the exception of some Chinese brands in China).

NFLX – Changed our usual visit to Blockbuster Video on Friday nights in anticipation of family time watching videos over the weekend. It also helped shape the future of entertainment around the world as we have begun moving away from cable to a more concierge approach to personal entertainment. NFLX is in every country around the world with the exception of Mainland China and North Korea.

V – Visa is still Visa, it wasn't so much a game changer as it was now everywhere, all over the world and has many facets to marketing plan such as the credit card, debit card, the gift card, the Apple iPhone swipe, and the pre-paid card. Also, Visa cards and/or applications are sent to hundreds of thousands, if not millions, of college students and graduates each year without fail. According to the National Center for Education Statistics, about 19.9 million students will attend universities this fall (2019). That's a lot, and each time a product of Visa is used, you as an owner get paid. (Back to School Statistics, 2019)

SBUX – When was the last time you walked or drove past a Starbucks establishment and there was not at least a 5-minute wait to get service. There are over 3,600 Starbucks shops in China alone. Somehow, Starbucks got it right and the world can't get enough of the wakeful concoctions of the brand. Around the world right now there are 29,865 stores in 78 different markets with a plan to grow at a rate of 6-7 percent annually. (MacLellan, 2019)

NKE – Nike is one of the most recognized brands in the entire world. With the world-wide coverage of sports, the Olympics, World Cup events, Championships, and bigger than life athletes, the "Just Do It" moniker and famous swoosh are bound to make a splash on the world of investing. Just like the cutting-edge footwear and clothing are making an impact as to winners and losers, the stock price continues its upward trend and continues to be the one to beat.

MCD – McDonald's is one of the world's largest holder of prime real estate valued at over $30 billion in over 32,000 locations around the world. The reason MCD is a game-changer is because it continues to re-invent itself as tastes (health concerns) change around the world. But what makes it really special is its consistency, and no matter what country you purchase the food in, it's always the same. (Purdy, 2017)

AMZN – This amazing company (concept) has put pressure on so many businesses over the recent past, that as a result, many of the giant brick-and-mortar companies have shut-down stores drastically or have gone out of business as a result. If you are realistic, you can see the landscape changing month by month and year by year. Soon the AMZN drones will fill the skies and certain packages will be delivered right to your door without ever being on a truck. Now AMZN owns Whole Foods, Ring, Zappos and many other movie and book companies and they are ready to continue to grow and compete! (Reiff, 2019)

BA – Boeing has had to battle against Airbus on a global scale in marketing, sales, and passenger comfort. The other competitors are so far behind they are not mentioned in the same conversation. But what makes Boeing a game-changer, the newest plane to fly, the 787 Dreamliner. Produced in three different sizes it may be the world's best airplane ever built as indicated by the number of orders over its rival the Airbus (1,398 versus 700) and the AB-350. When there are only two competitors, it's hard to go wrong with your investment!

Microsoft took computing from the office to your home, and eventually on the road with the laptop. It definitely changed everything. Mastercard is very much like Visa in its convenience and accessibility to money when you need it. AutoZone and the other auto parts stores all have done well due to the financial crisis' that continue to plague the country and causes many people to not buy new but fix the cars they already own. Facebook totally changed the way we interact with one another and allowed us as a world to get in contact and stay in contact with those we care about. Lockheed Martin will continue to be a game-changer as we continue to explore outer-space and develop new defense technologies in the face of new and more creative threats. Chipotle is always packed due to the game-changing trend away from GMOs and America's fascination with farm-to-table cuisine. Keurig (GMCR) totally change the way we make and drink coffee. As coffee pots come and go, I think this one is here to stay.

On the other hand, Vail Resorts has been around forever, so what makes them so different. They have been buying properties all over the place for the past few years. They own Vail, CO; Beaver Creek, Breckenridge, and Keystone in CO; Park City and Canyons in Utah; Heavenly, NorthStar, and Kirkwood in Lake Tahoe, CA; Perisher in Australia, Wilmot Mountain in Wisconsin, and others around the world and on the east coast of North America. (Burke, 2019)

Home Depot is a mainstay along with its nearest competitor, Lowes. They have the lion's share of home improvement traffic and sales for large or small projects around the house or office. It doesn't take rocket science to tell you that these are sustainable businesses and they will continue to track in a positive direction for years to come! Home Depot is not necessarily a game-changer but a sustainer.

In conclusion, it's always better to buy the game-changers because they are helping to formulate our future, whether in what we eat, wear, drink, drive, or use to solve complex problems; they will grow and continue to flourish. Find your own game-changers. My 18-year old son told me about EA Sports, and it might be a good idea to invest in on-line gaming in 2010. My wife even paid for a subscription for him to participate in on-line gaming, and he showed me the charts. But because I knew nothing about on-line gaming, I didn't buy the stock; it blew up! People are now playing on national TV (ESPN) and competing for $1 million for the winner. The stock went from ~$11/share (2011) to over ~$140/share (2017) over a three-year period, but I didn't listen, so I missed the opportunity (an annual compound interest rate of 114.5%). So, when he told me about a vegan restaurant that served the best hamburgers and cheeseburgers that he has ever tasted, all I asked him to do was to bring me one of the burgers. He said that people start lining up to buy the burgers around 3:20-3:30 pm in order to be near the front of the line when the place opened at 4:00 pm. He decided to buy me a burger one day so I could taste it, and the rest they say is history. I agreed with his assessment of the taste and the next morning, I purchased Beyond Meat (BYND) for $130/share. A month later the price of the stock had risen to over $239/share (a 54 percent increase) in only one and a half months. I believe BYND is a game-changer.

Diversification

According to Warren Buffett, risk tolerance drives diversification strategy. Modern portfolio theory defines the benefit of diversification as a mitigation to price volatility. In other words, the more diverse your stock holdings are the less you are affected when a few of them move in a negative direction. Warren Buffett on the other hand, believes that concentrating on a few choice companies that you are familiar with will raise your intensity as you think about the business and the comfort level you must feel with its economic characteristics before buying the stock. In other words, if you know and understand the businesses you are buying, you will pay attention to them because of your familiarity and use. You can then study them and follow them closely and understand their true value. According to Buffett, "The more knowledge you have about your company, the less risk you are taking." (Hagstrom R. G., 2005)

To make this as easy as possible, think of the things you already buy and places where you use their services, such as name brand items and restaurants you may frequent. How about which shoe brand you wear or the car you drive. Which type of oil and gas do you prefer to use in your vehicles and what perfume do you like the most. Other things that may go on your list are what do my neighbors buy a lot of and what are my children constantly going on about. Think about all the things you have to have in your life, and you can't really do without such as your cell phone (brand?), laptop, computer, or smart device. Do you like one fast-food chain more than another or are they all equal in your opinion. Finally, think about where we are going as a whole world, a nation, and as a family. That means think about what's being legalized and what's being talked up as the next big thing. With some forethought you will be able to come up with a list of 10-20 items or services that are critical to your life and to your future.

This will be your starter list and where you will begin shopping for stocks. Some of those stocks may very well be some of the ones mentioned in the Game-Changers section. You should feel free to add and remove stocks to your watch list as you choose but keep in mind that you know these companies because you already spend your money on them. A friend of mine called me one day to ask about Soda Stream (SODA), to see if we should sell the shares, we had bought 12-months earlier. I ask him why and he stated, "Because I'm in Lowes and there are a bunch of them in the corner with a 30 percent off sale price on them." We sold the shares the next day and two weeks later we heard Soda Stream was shopping their company looking for a buyer. The price of the stock went down shortly thereafter, and we were able to preserve some of our profits before the price fell.

Once you have a list, you have to decide which stocks to purchase first (see "Chapter 12 When to Buy") and how much to spend. To make the list easier to diversify, divide the list into categories: Communications, Consumer Discretionary, Consumer Staples, Energy, Financials, Healthcare, Industrials, Information Technology, Materials, Real Estate, and Utilities are the largest eleven sectors of the stock market. For 2019 Bank of America has a list of one stock from each sector they thought would do well in 2019:

Here are Bank of America's top stock picks for each sector:

- Communication services: Walt Disney Co. (ticker: DIS)

- Consumer discretionary: General Motors Co. (GM)

- Consumer staples: Molson Coors Brewing Co. (TAP)

- Energy: Exxon Mobil Corp. (XOM)

- Financials: Morgan Stanley (MS)

- Health care: CVS Health Corp. (CVS)

- Industrials: Raytheon Co. (RTN)

- Information technology: Microsoft Corp. (MSFT)

- Materials: International Paper Co. (IP)

- Real estate: Simon Property Group (SPG)

- Utilities: Public Service Enterprise Group (PEG)

(Duggan, 2019)

It's my opinion you will have better insight and understanding if you pick those companies that you already are familiar with initially. After you have experienced success with those then you should be able to branch out some into things recommended by your financial advisor and or financial planner.

CHAPTER 12

WHEN TO BUY?

"Those who master money are free to serve others still mastered by it." – **Orrin Woodward, author**

"To every thing there is a season, and a time to every purpose under the heaven:" Ecclesiastes 3:1

Bear Market – Buy When the Overall Market Goes Down

It's December 19, 2018, and the stock market continues its downward trend. The pressure on the market, according to the pundits on CNBC, has to do with an increase in the interest rates by the Federal Reserve, Great Britain uncertainty as it approaches BREIX, thousands of layoffs for GM and Ford, and tariff war with China that has had global implications. Also, many investors are apprehensive due to many Trump cabinet members and lawyers being indicted for covering up hush money payments to protect the Republican candidate!

The nervousness in the air seems to be more reactionary, but none-the-less, the market seems to be in a vertical slide in the wrong direction. My personal gains for the year have gone from a high of (+) 57.8 percent in July, to a modest (+) 22.0 percent on December 19, 2018. This is probably better than most, although no one wants to see their portfolio drop this much over a few months! I was not worried because market corrections and drops are all a part of my overall investment strategy.

The beauty of the matter is, it was the perfect time to purchase shares of any company you had your eyes on. A lot of stocks were at their 52-week lows, some were creating new lows, and several companies were buying back stock at an enormous rate. The chart below shows where the market closed at 4:00 PM (EST), on December 19, 2018. A day like this makes a lot of people run for the hills (gold stocks, bonds, cash, and treasuries, etc.), but for me, I just got excited to find the bargains for the stocks I already owned.

STOCKS
DECEMBER 19

NASDAQ		6,636.83
NASDAQ Co...		-147.08
NYSE		11,371.84
NYSE COM...		-130.32
Dow Jones		23,323.66
Dow Jones I...		-351.98
S&P 500		2,506.96
S&P 500		-39.20
QQQ		154.53
Invesco QQ...		-3.89

BUSINESS NEWS

No one seemed to know what to do, but it was a perfect time to enter the market. Warren Buffett says, to be brave and bold when everyone else is running away! A great indication of when to buy stocks is usually when a company buys its own stocks. Let's face it, who knows a company's financial health better than the company itself.

It is important to note if this massive drop was not the bottom for the bear run on the market, nothing really made sense on the macro scale. Unemployment was at an all-time low, most businesses reported significant profits, corporate tax rates were lower, and a steadily growing economy should have shown an upturn in the fundamentals! The opposite seemed to be true.

(Finance, 2019)

Looking at the chart, the red circle shows where the market was on December 19, 2018. It wasn't long afterwards that new money flowed into the market and it began a fast recovery that lasted until June 2019, followed by a rise and another drop in early August 2019. A large drop in stock prices signals a chance to purchase stocks at a discount, because the thing to remember here, is if the overall economy is doing well, the market will continue to trend up.

I bought as much stock as I could each time a sale was triggered, which increased my total number of shares.

An article from Bloomberg says:

> "The real issue is the three things markets have been focused on are coming to a head at one time: an aggressive Fed raising rates, fears of a global growth slowdown, and the trade war with China," Cliff Hodge, director of investments at Cornerstone Wealth, said in an interview. "Compounding that is the political headlines regarding the government shutdown. It's all hitting us, all at the same time and is causing a major shift in risk-off sentiment." (Herron, 2018)

So, buy when the whole market drops. How do you do this with confidence? Remember we are in this for the long haul and although you might miss the very bottom, the market's general trend over time is up. It's like buying a Louis Vuitton on sale!

Sector Madness – Buy When A Sector Of The Economy Is Depressed

Sometimes there is bad news in a particular sector of the economy such as the transportation industrial complex in the aftermath of 9-11. Airlines in the United States and around the world were affected as air travel slowed to a trickle as a result of the devastating effects of the crisis. Shortly after, some of the airlines emerged from bankruptcy; their stock prices suffered and were selling well below their intrinsic value due to fear, and the uncertainty surrounding their ability to regain global prominence after the security. I was able to purchase United Airlines (UAL) stock at a low price of $2.89/share (its high after bankruptcy was near $55/share), because of the some of the factors mentioned above. It didn't make sense that a company that had reorganized, lowered its overall out-flow of cash, and eliminated employee and vendor contracts, should be selling at such a discount. After a few months the price began to rise, and I eventually sold the stock when it went above $12.50 a share. The same thing happened to banks like Goldman Sachs after the housing crisis, and to high-tech companies such as Apple after the tech bubble burst.

This technique is about paying attention to what is going on around you and not being afraid when things look bad. It's like shopping at your favorite shoe store when they are having a half-off sale. Most people will sell all of their posi-tions in the stock market after it has dropped significantly, due to the fear they will lose everything. But the key is to do the opposite. If you purchased a great stock like Apple for instance at $130 a share, but due to the tech bubble problem the price is now dropping towards $79 a share; do you sell or buy. I encourage you to resist the temptation to try to salvage your paper losses by selling and making the losses perma-nent. Instead buy the stock as it drops (because you know Apple is an amazing company and will eventually recover from any issue) in segments. If you have $10,000 to spend, then use half of the money ($5000) after a 10-20 percent drop to lower you cost basis of the stock you already own. If the price of stock continues to drop, buy again if it continues down another 10-15 percent, (spending half of what you have remaining in cash) spend another $2,500. Because no one knows when the price will bottom-out, you can only react to what the market gives you. Eventually, the price of a great company will stabilize, and everyone will want to get in on the action when it begins to return to its true value (~$130/ share). By this point you have already established your stock positions for the long haul and will reap the benefits of money returning to the market. (See chart below)

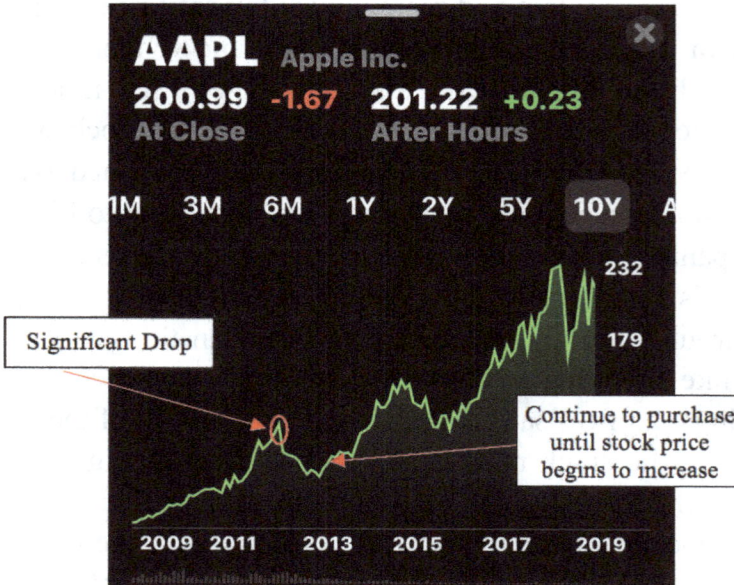

In the case of Apple. the stock price from 2013 exceeded the original high at the beginning of the significant drop. There are many similar cases of a company in a particular sector experiencing a temporary setback before returning to its proper valuation. It is to your advantage if you can recognize the issue and take advantage of it before it's too late. If you miss it, there will be other opportunities, so don't be too hard on yourself, because it takes a lot of practice to go against the grain. Remember: "...Be bold when everyone else is afraid, and afraid when everyone else is bold." – Warren Buffett

Bad News – Buy when a great company delivers news that, on the surface, seems "bad"

Netflix used to only charge one price for all their combined services. But on September 11, 2011, the Wallstreet Journal reported the following:

> Netflix Inc. NFLX -2.21%_'s move to separate its movie-streaming business and its DVD-by-mail service failed to soothe many customers' anger over the company's recent price increase. Netflix Chief Executive Reed Hastings announced the split in a blog post Sunday night, saying the move was the undisclosed impetus for a recent price increase that outraged customers and sent the company's stock price plummeting. He apologized for not having given the explanation sooner. (Smith, 2011)

This was bad news for customers and the price of Netflix stock plummeted to a new low of sub-$70 per share from a then high of $170 per share. But if you recalled Mr. Hastings went on to indicate the company was moving towards the future and it was his way of ensuring the future success of Netflix on a global scale. The article also stated:

> The change effectively raised many subscribers' monthly charge by 60%, to $16 from $10. Last week, in light of negative reaction to the price increases, the company cut its subscriber forecast by one million, or 4%. In response, Netflix's share price plummeted 19%. Mr. Hastings's explanation for the price changes and the company's failure to explain its impetus took on an introspective tone.

"Inside Netflix I say, 'Actions speak louder than words,' and we should just keep improving our service," he wrote. But he added, "I should have personally given a full justification to our members" for the price increases. (Smith, 2011)

I was so convinced that he was on the right track, but it was not because of what he said but, because my children were always watching and talking about Netflix. The problem was, we didn't have Netflix. So, I asked them how they were watching it, they explained how they could use one of their friend's sign-on (each subscription came with five). When the price dropped, I started systematically buying the stock until it went down to $63 per share. Why not, my children were willing to use other people's subscriptions in order to watch this new way of entertainment. I was not disappointed (see below).

Prices reflect a 1:7 split on 7/11/2015

Since I purchased the stock in 2011 it has skyrocketed, because it not only had bad news, but it is a great company poised to be a game-changer. Remember to buy when everyone else is selling if it is a company you believe in and want to own for a long time. Over time you will be able to reap great rewards. Since its IPO, NFLX price has increased over 32,000 percent over the past 17 years.

Once you know it's a great company, be poised to buy on bad news such as missed revenues, projected new subscribers, or missed earnings per share. Many times, the short-sightedness of the market will create tremendous buying opportunities that should never be ignored. For example, at the writing of this book Netflix had just missed its own projected forecast for the second quarter of 5.2 million new subscribers (world-wide). Instead the numbers came in as 2.7 million and the stock free-fell to $307 per share from $385 in just a week. Other factors weighing on the price were new competitions from Disney, CBS, and other streaming services making announcements. The content war was also in full swing as Disney stated it was pulling its content from the Netflix platform eventually and the popular shows "Friends and The Office" would also be taken off Netflix.

Hearing this you may consider, why hold onto, or buy Netflix, with all the supposed negative information floating around? Remember Warren Buffett said a great company is known around the world and seemingly recession-proof. (Hagstrom R. , 2005) Well, NFLX is in every country except North Korea and Mainland China, with over 150 million subscribers and growing daily. Also, shortly after the subscription miss, Reed Hastings stated on television that the missed 2.5 million subscriptions will show up in the third quarter, boosting its subscription total by 7 million new subscribers. (Burch, 2019)

With the proper knowledge and understanding you could now purchase a stock like Netflix at this lower price, while expecting a great increase in its price in the third quarter. If you think long term, you may consider this an opportunity to lower your cost basis if you had purchased it above $375 a share. Either way, bad news is not always "bad news."

Dividend Payout – Buy When A Company Pays A Dividend

When a company pays a dividend, the price of the stock will usually drop to reflect the lower Market Capitalization due to the cash being paid to the shareholders. If most of the shareholders of the company participate in dividend re-investment however, the money will flow back into the stock price and this will reflect the activity as an increase. This is a measure I used when the market was in turmoil in 2007-2008 and the only stocks that were holding their own were McDonalds and Walmart. I noticed that the price remained in the same $2-3 range, but it was at the lower end during the dividend payout period and would move up three to four days after the dividends were re-invested. It may be a small move, but the dividend play kept my portfolio from falling any lower than a negative (-) 24 percent during the crisis and gave it a 1-2 percent boost each quarter.

IPO – Buy A Great Company During An IPO

While sitting in my master's class at Regis University in 2007, Visa announced an initial public offering (IPO) estimated to be $37-42 per share. They actually raised $17 Billion in the offering, becoming the largest IPO in history.

> Visa Inc, the world's largest credit card network, filed with regulators on Friday to raise up to $10 billion in an initial public offering, in one of the

largest and most eagerly awaited U.S. stock offer-
ings. Visa has said it plans to use IPO proceeds
to fund expansion and an escrow account to help
cover legal bills. The network and MasterCard face
a variety of antitrust lawsuits from rivals and retail-
ers, some of which accuse them of price fixing.

Visa's roots date to 1958 when a Bank of America Corp (BAC.N) predecessor created the blue,
white and gold Bank Ameri-card, helping pave the
way for the modern credit card business. That card
has evolved into Visa. MasterCard went public in
May 2006 in a $2.4 billion IPO and its shares have
since risen roughly five-fold. (Feldt, 2007)

In my mind I thought they were already publicly traded,
but after a little research I knew they would go the way of
Mastercard. After looking at the growth demonstrated by
Mastercard it was a "no brainer." As I sat at my computer,
I input my trades for the next day with the appropriate trade
limits and my classmates questioned my actions as foolish,
and a few, "You may lose your shirt." The next day my
trades executed, and I was on my way with just a few hundred shares. I was confident it would pay off. Two weeks
later my classmates asked me how my gamble paid off? I
proudly opened my account and showed them the new stock
price was climbing past $72.50; I was no longer a joke, but
a genius in their eyes. From that moment on I became the
leader in their eyes and appointed classroom CEO for the
next two years as we completed our advanced degrees.

Not every IPO works out right away like Visa, some
never get off the ground, and others zoom up between 3-5
times their IPO price only to come down after the company

fails to produce expected profits. I took advantage of several IPOs over the past few years such as Tesla (TSLA), Facebook (FB), HUYA, Iqiyi (IQ), Square (SQ), Lyft (LYFT), and Uber (UBER), to name a few of them. Some have turned out great, the others are too early to tell. Although I was late to the Chipotle (CMG) IPO, I eventually woke up to realize the trend towards farm-to-table restaurants and bought CMG after it had hit over $200 a share.

How do you know if the IPO you are considering is a great company? Use the "Common Man Traits of an IPO Test" by way of Warren Buffett:

1. Do I understand the business?
2. Do I buy the products or services?
3. Do other people I know buy their products or services?
4. Is it a company of the future versus the past?
5. What will sustain the future of this company?
6. Is there something special that distinguishes this company from others?
7. Is the company international or has international potential?
8. Will the company be able to withstand competition?
9. Are young people customers of this company?
10. Will the company be profitable?

If you can answer yes to more than seven of these questions, it is a "buy" the IPO kind of situation. Less than seven years and I would probably wait until after the initial two to three months after the IPO to let the volatility and excitement ebb. After the initial period is over a calmness usually ensues and the price changes and growth become more predictable.

Anytime Is A Good Time – These Stocks Can Be Bought Anytime

Some stocks took off after the IPO and they have never really had more than a stagnant quarter or two over the life of the stock. For example; Visa (V), Amazon (AMZN), Intuit (INTU), Salesforce (CRM), The Trade Desk (TTD), and Paycom Software (PAYC) to name a few. There are many others that demonstrate the ability to withstand the ups and downs of a volatile market and a shaky economy. What they have in common seems to be the necessity of their products or services. On your list of the things you cannot do without in your life, try to identify those things that are completely necessary for you and others and you have a start to your "buy anytime list."

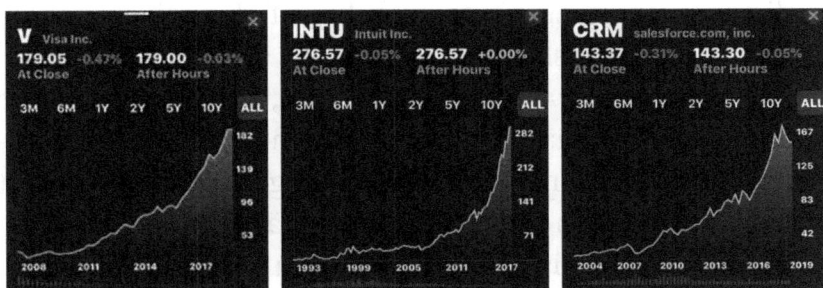

My list is definitely different than that of my children and of my wife, but if you have joint accounts with others your combined list should include items from all shareholders. I don't have a need for makeup, perfume, or fancy shoes, but these are legitimate "buy anytime" stocks.

The few that come to mind are: Estee Lauder (EL), Brown & Brown (BRO), and Louis Vuitton (LVMH).

These companies from your list should be some of the first stocks you actually purchase because there are no secret formulas as to when you should buy. My children all have

Visa stock because between my wife and I, we have probably 10-12 Visa cards for our personal and business lives. So, the first stock they have is Visa and it would seem they can't get enough of those Apple products, and that is the second stock they all have. If you were to breakdown the Visa phenomenon, it makes total sense this stock should be in most, if not all portfolios. So, make you list and start your investments off with the sure things in your life.

Stock Split – Buy Great Companies When The Stock Splits

When you had to split something as a kid, that generally didn't feel like a perk. But when you're an investor, splitting can be a good thing. Stock splits are a way a company's board of directors can increase the number of shares outstanding while lowering the share price.

For example, in a 2-for-1 stock split, an additional share is given for each share held by a shareholder. So, if a company had 10 million shares outstanding before the split, it will have 20 million shares outstanding after a 2-for-1 split.

A stock's price is also affected by a stock split. After a split, the stock price will be reduced since the number of shares outstanding has increased. In the example of a 2-for-1 split, the share price will be halved. Thus, although the number of outstanding shares and the price change, the market capitalization remains constant. (Beers, 2019)

The sound of splitting sounds bad unless you are talking about stocks. What I have witnessed with the great companies is that the stock prices can grow until it makes it tough for new investors to buy the shares because the price is so high. Warren Buffett's company stock, Berkshire Hathaway

"A" stock, is trading at greater than $300,000 per share. I still remember when it was $25,000 a share and I felt, I'll never be able to afford that stock, well I was wrong, but it is still expensive! Warren Buffett has decided for now not to split the stock. But he did split his B-shares at a ratio of 50:1 and the stock price changed from $5000/share to $50 overnight. At the time I had 30 shares of the BRK-B stock, and after the split I had 1500 shares at $50/share. The value was the same but now the risk of owning the stock seemed less. Shortly after the split, the price of the stock began to rise at 15-20 percent a year, and I found myself feeling pretty good about making the decision to buy an additional 1500 shares after the split. Now my total holdings for BRK-B were valued at over $300,000 because the stock price had grown to over $100/share. It was the first time I ever owned anything valued at over a quarter-million dollars. BRK-B is now trading at $200 per share.

A stock split creates its own buying frenzy amongst those individuals wanting to buy, but not being able to afford the stock before the split. What's nice about a stock split is if you own the stock already, you don't have to do anything but watch it grow. You can also take advantage of the split using it to own more shares of a good thing; a great company! You are an owner! With my goal being 1 million shares of all the companies I own, the stock split serves a great purpose in my strategy for making money work for me. The first time I experienced a surprised split was Visa. One day I saw a steep drop of the price of Visa; I had dropped 50 percent in one day. I was shocked and started investigating and found that I now had over 800 shares versus ~200 (March 19, 2019). Visa had a 4:1 stock split; what a nice surprise! I quickly bought another 200 hundred shares and now had 1000 shares of Visa in my portfolio. The new price after the split was $65.41 and that was more affordable than $271 a share. Soon the price moved upwards and created more profits and more opportunity. The stock is now trading at ~$180 per share; what a great run!

CHAPTER 13

WHEN TO SELL

"Never spend your money before you have it."
– Thomas Jefferson, third president of the United States

"So they took the money, and did as they were taught:"
Matthew 28:15

It has never been my goal to play the stock market, because it feels and sounds like gambling when I hear it being spoken about this way. Warren Buffett states you should own stocks in companies you already buy goods and services from instead those you have no clue about. In other words, stay away from "hot tips," those stocks you heard someone got rich overnight by jumping into right away. My goal on the other hand has always been to accumulate as many shares as possible of all the companies I "own." If you think of yourself as an owner you will take a different approach to what, when, and how much of a particular stock you purchase. If I can own a million plus shares of all the companies I own, not only would I be rich, but my children, nor their children's children would ever want for money. They could spend their time on helping others and ensuring the future of our world was intact versus working for money!

Take A Little Off The Top

Sometimes a stock will surprise you and spike upwards at such a rate that seems too good to be true. In one day NFLX went up $72, I could have been extremely happy but really it was too good to be true. Well in the case of NFLX it wasn't. As it turned out, NFLX went on to surpass that high point and eventually topped $700 per share. At the time I felt compelled to sell one-third of my holdings, even though greed was saying don't do it. My greed wanted to cheer and get excited about the growth and my good fortune, but instead my cooler side prevailed and I sold a third of my holdings. That was a really great profit, that was moved from the hypothetical of a paper gain to an actual cash gain that I thought I would use to buy other stock. Instead the price of NFLX fell over the next few days and I ended up using the money to buy even more shares of NFLX, using the same money I had cashed in just a week and a half earlier. Because the stock price dropped, I was able to add an additional 6 percent more shares than I had before without having to add any more money to my account.

Stock	Number of Shares	Price of Shares	Price Total/ Increase/ Drop	New Price
NFLX (Nov 1)	1000	$250	$72	$322
Sold NFLX	333	$322	$107,226	
NFLX (Nov 15)	667	$272	$50	
Bought NFLX	395	$272	New shares total	1062 Shares

- Started with 1000 shares of NFLX.

- Sold 333 shares of NFLX on Nov 1 for $322/share for a total of $107,226.

- Price of NFLX dropped by $50 to $272/share.

- Bought 395 shares of NFLX for $107,226.

- Ended with 1062 shares of NFLX (6 percent increase in shares without adding any cash).

- A month later the stock price was higher back above $322 a $20,000 gain in less than two months.

I thought this was a fluke, but what I found out totally by mistake, was a lot of times the price of a stock will overshoot its intrinsic value only to return to something more reasonable. Then it will eventually return to the previously tested high point and exceed it. Remember we are only interested in great companies that meet our criteria. The stocks of these companies exhibit this type of behavior when there is "good news." Most people were buying at the time of the good news, but I went in the opposite direction and received an additional 6 percent gain in a short period of time using several different techniques in conjunction with each other. The results reminded me of what Buffett said about selling when others are greedy. Don't let greed stop you from taking a profit.

Better Choice

Sometimes you may have to sell a stock when there is a better choice. I shop at Lowes (LOWE) and Home Depot (HD). I bought stocks in both companies at the same time because I could not decipher the benefits of one stock over the other. Eventually, Home Depot won out because of the consistency of its price growth which was due to the management and customer service teams around the country.

I did the same thing with Lockheed Martin (LMT), Raytheon (RTN), and Northrop Grumman (NOC) and eventually settled on LMT due to the difference in dividends.

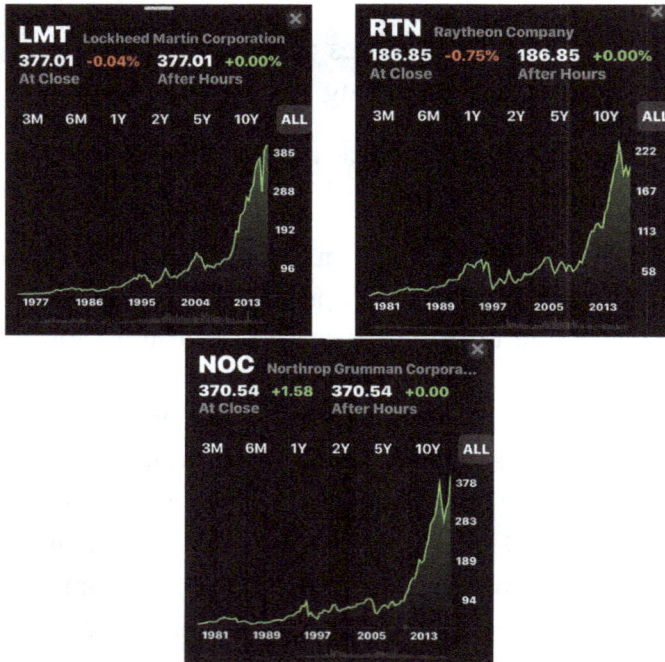

The charts are almost identical to one another, but what is not shown is the dividends being paid. LMT pays out $2.20 per share per quarter, RTN pays $0.94 per quarter, and NOC pays $1.32 per quarter. Because the companies were all in the defense sector and were all moving in concert with each other, it was an easy choice plus it allowed me to have a lot more shares of LMT. This means I began collecting more dividends each quarter and those dividends were being compounded each year as well as the increase in the price of the stock. With 1000 shares of LMT it means I would get $2200 worth of shares re-invested in the first quarter, equating to an increase of almost 6 shares, which means the following quarter I would get another 6 shares added to my portfolio of LMT. By the end of the year my account compounded and had an approximate total of 1023 shares of LMT by just owning the stock; a $8700 gain because of the compounding effect of the quarterly dividend.

Remember "It's not rocket science, it's just math."

Playing with "Their Money" – How to Play With "House Money"

Although I am not a gambler, one of my favorite sayings is "I'm playing with house money!" That concept happens when a gambler wins enough to double the initial investment, takes that amount and puts it away to not be used. At this point in the scenario, the gambler is using his winnings to advance his overall cash stash. The same is true in stock trading and portfolio building. If I purchase 100 shares of a company and the price doubles over a period of time (my goal is usually 1-3 years), I may sell half of the stock and used the proceeds to invest in other great companies (diversification), or just let it remain in cash in case of a market downturn in order to re-purchase the same stock at a lower price (see "Take a Little Off the Top" above.) Using this technique, I have been able to increase the number of great companies I own to over twenty-five which is more than enough for a diverse portfolio. You really only need approximately 7-15 stocks to achieve this, but as the stocks that I owned doubled in value, I felt more compelled to branch out to those other companies on my list that were also doing well.

As each stock reached the 100 percent or doubling point, I still made the move to at least sell 50 percent, and sometimes I was reluctant to do so. I didn't always follow my own advice. I got caught up like everyone else and let the process wash over me without actually taking effect. After each encounter I found that the process was the actual thing that was successful, not me. My wife's aunt from Chicago always said you have TO MAKE A PLAN AND THEN WORK YOUR PLAN. The problem most of us have is, we don't really have a plan to begin with. How could we? With the little to no financial literacy we have it's a blessing not to be totally in debt with no money saved for a rainy day. But I learned how to trust the plan and the process, and they have served me well. For the past eleven years my compounded returns have averaged greater than 30 percent and all the techniques are in this book.

Happy Feelings – Take Some Profits When You Start To Feel Good

If you ever feel super happy that your stocks are zooming upwards, its probably a good idea to sell between 3-5 percent of your holdings because your feelings are usually shared by everyone else. If you are disciplined in this technique you will be able to take advantage of those quirky and quick market drops that appear out of nowhere (midnight tweet perhaps) and disappear as though they never happen. On August 5, 2019, a tweet extending the China trade war, sent the market reeling to a DOW 700-point loss and an over 2 percent loss in the NASDQ. By Wednesday the 7th, the market corrected and returned within a percent of its previous highs. Just before the drop I was feeling happy, but I did not sell that 3-5 percent and subsequently missed out on a grand opportunity. Fortunately for me I had a few dollars in cash that I was able to purchase a small number of great stocks at an excellent discount!

No matter what you do, never sell a great company when the price drops. All you are doing is locking in an actual loss. Most experts agree with Warren Buffett to be bold when others are afraid, but its tougher to put into practice. The final piece of the puzzle is to avoid emotional risk, the chance that you'll end up selling when stocks fall. For many people, having a conflict-free financial adviser is the solution. (Puritz, 2019)

CHAPTER 14

I DON'T HAVE ANY MONEY TO INVEST

"Without financial literacy, divorce rates soar, families rupture, and women stay with abusive men for financial security. A lack of jobs contributes to riots and illegal activity. Name any situation and it goes back to money. We need to focus on poverty eradication." – **John Hope Bryant, financial literacy entrepreneur and businessman**

"The people of the land have used oppression, and exercised robbery, and have vexed the poor and needy."
Ezekiel 22:29

I hear the words, "I don't have any money to invest" more often than you could ever imagine. But if you just take the time to think about it, you have the money, you just have to want a brighter future more than your temporary pleasure. Many times, our habits and inefficient use of resources deny us the foresight of opportunity lost! What I mean by this is if I buy a cup of Starbucks coffee on a daily basis, I may spend anywhere from \$2-5 dollars a day, \$10-25 dollars a week, and as much as \$100 per month. Its not that you shouldn't drink coffee, but if you also want to have a financial future, you have to make a few sacrifices now to enjoy your life even more in the future. What if you like to eat out? If you pay \$15 dollars for lunch each day the numbers add up to over \$300 per month and by combining this with the coffee you drink each morning, you definitely have some money to invest if you choose. There are probably several things you can do to cut a few costs that are considered luxury/enjoyable but not necessary and so forth, but balance is important. Don't cut out all pleasures but do pare them down to give yourself funds for investing.

The other important point here is to consider not using credit cards or at least make sure you pay them off each month to avoid the interest charges. There is nothing wrong with using credit, but it has to be done responsibly (See Chapter 6 – First Things First). If you understood the math behind the high interest rates paid on credit cards you will run from having a balance greater than one month. Take for instance a credit card with a \$20,000 balance:

Credit Card Balance	**20,000**
Interest Rate (%)	**18.5**

Minimum payment is percentage of the balance or minimum amount, whichever is higher.

Minimum Percentage	interest + 1%
Minimum Amount	**200**

Reset	Calculate

Pay off Months:	**154**
Total Interest:	**23,025.46**
Total Payment:	**43,025.46**

According to the calculations it will take over twelve and a half years to pay off the credit card, and that is without ever making any further purchases. You end up paying over $23,000 in interest rate fees and a total of $43,000 for a few months of frivolous spending. It's not worth it!

401K Magic/Tax Implications

There is a way to help fund your 401K and other investment plans using money that would normally all go to taxes. A recent article in USA today outlined a plan that I had been teaching for years to people to help maximize their 401Ks. If you increase your deductions over time to reach the IRS limit ($19,000 for 2019), you will use money that would normally go to pay federal and state taxes. It's not a one-for-one match but it will help you reach the max goal if you make a salary large enough to put $1583 away each month. Because the money going to the 401K is pre-tax money, it will lower the amount you actually pay in taxes. The article states:

> If your 401(k) balance is skimpier than it should be at your age, now's the time to "bump up" the percentage of your pay that is invested in your retirement savings account, says Mark Lamkin, CEO and chief market strategist at Lamkin Wealth Management in Louisville, Kentucky. The maximum amount you can set aside in your 401(k) in 2019 under IRS rules is $19,000 and workers 50 and older can save $6,000 more in so-called catch-up contributions. The limit on annual IRA contributions is $6,000, with allowable catch-up contributions of $1,000 if you are 50 or older. To work toward maxing out, Lamkin advises people

to gradually increase your paycheck deductions, if possible, to the percentage that boosts your annual savings to the IRS limit. (Shell, 2019)

To accomplish this, you will have to re-submit your W4 to your company, either to the HR administrator or online if that is an option. As a rough calculation, each deduction you add in the form of a "dependent" will put another $120-140 in your pay check. But you have to make sure to increase your contribution to the 401K by an equal amount. For example, if your check increases by $700, after you figured out the percentage of your pay check deductions to gain the increased net $700 then change your contribution amount to include the newly released funds.

Mark's Salary (40 years old): $10,500/month

Current W4: Married and 4
 Current 401K Contribution: 7% ($735/month)
 Additional $848/month needed to max 401K

 Taxable Income After Deductions: ~ $86,000

 Tax Bracket: 22% (~$1560/month depending on additional deductions)

New W4: Married and 12
 New 401K Contribution: 14% ($1428/month)
 Additional $155/month needed to max 401K

 Taxable Income After Deductions: ~$77,200

 Tax Bracket: 12% (~$778/month depending on additional deductions)

At this point Mark can choose to increase his contributions which could max his 401K. As it stands, he was able to significantly increase his contributions without sacrificing his take-home pay and at the same time lowered his overall tax burden.

The difference a few dollars make in the chart below in Mark's retirement will be an additional $600-700,000 by using this 401K contribution strategy (see below).

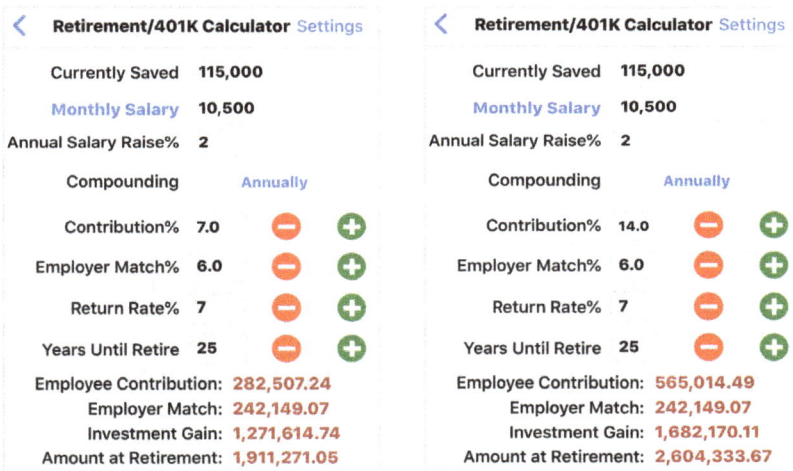

Retirement/401K Calculator Settings	
Currently Saved	115,000
Monthly Salary	10,500
Annual Salary Raise%	2
Compounding	Annually
Contribution%	7.0 ⊖ ⊕
Employer Match%	6.0 ⊖ ⊕
Return Rate%	7 ⊖ ⊕
Years Until Retire	25 ⊖ ⊕
Employee Contribution:	282,507.24
Employer Match:	242,149.07
Investment Gain:	1,271,614.74
Amount at Retirement:	1,911,271.05

Retirement/401K Calculator Settings	
Currently Saved	115,000
Monthly Salary	10,500
Annual Salary Raise%	2
Compounding	Annually
Contribution%	14.0 ⊖ ⊕
Employer Match%	6.0 ⊖ ⊕
Return Rate%	7 ⊖ ⊕
Years Until Retire	25 ⊖ ⊕
Employee Contribution:	565,014.49
Employer Match:	242,149.07
Investment Gain:	1,682,170.11
Amount at Retirement:	2,604,333.67

Richest Man Syndrome – Don't Try To Impress Others At The Expense Of Your Finances

After reading "The Millionaire Next Door," I took on some of the traits, characteristics, and habits those mentioned. I stopped buying new cars. I put large down payments on the cars I did purchase with the intention of paying them off in three years or less. I decided not to rent but own a modest home in a great neighborhood. I began using credit with caution. I cooked more, ate out less, and only bought expensive coffee occasionally. The problem is life is not that simple, and before I knew it my baptism of fire was upon me (see Chapter 3). After going through that melee the last thing on my mind was impressing people that either didn't know me or didn't care. Stay focused on your goals and those of your family and this problem of "Keeping up with the Joneses" goes away.

Just Do It

The biggest problem with any great endeavor is getting started! You have to either do it yourself or get some help to do it (i.e. financial advisors-fiduciary preferred). Make the decision to get started and set your plan. Once you have armed yourself with knowledge and understanding you can commence to implement the plan. It is imperative that you get started without delay no matter the amount you have to invest. It could be as little as $50 a month or as much as $5000 a month, regardless GET STARTED! Procrastination is relentless and does its job quite well. It is up to you to make sure procrastination doesn't win at all.

- Make everything automatic by working with your bank and set-up automatic withdrawals and contributions to all your savings and investments (no matter the amount).

- Decide on and purchase several books (Amazon works well) that will help educate you on all aspects of investing or at least as much as you think you need.

- Make an electronic list of all the companies you and your family decided upon and put them in your "Stocks" app on your phone.

- If you don't already have one, find a fiduciary financial advisor to help ease you into a trading platform that you can easily navigate. I prefer Schwab.com, but there are many others.

- Start by making your first purchase (if you don't have enough money for your first share, you may have to save up a few months).

- The next step is to pick at least 5 different stocks (companies) that you want to own and over the next few months buy 5 shares of each. If you have the money, then start by purchasing 10-20 shares each.

- Check your stock app each morning, takes about sixty seconds to find out what's going on with the market.

  o If the market is up significantly, until you have 100 shares you may want to just smile.

  o If the market is down significantly, it may be a good time to increase your holdings.

- Slowly add to your share total until you have 100 shares of each company using the techniques outlined in this book.

- Add to the different companies over time until you have a portfolio of 10-20 stocks that you are familiar with.

- After a while, you will start getting better at determining what to buy, when to buy, what to buy, and when to sell (if at all). Don't worry because if you have been reading and following along in this book, it will become as natural as breathing.

- By this point you will have a pretty good grasp on the process and the techniques, so review the plan as often as you need to and continue to add to your position (or sell) until you have 1000 or more shares of each company you own. The rest will be up to you!

- Remember at any time you can hire a Certified Financial Planner (CFP) to help you with your new-found wealth.

If you really want to see your money work for you, you have to spend time educating yourself on efficient tax strategies. One-third of your finances are dependent on how well you understand and can effectively implement tax strategies! This will not be covered in this book but will be published at a later date under a separate series entitled: "Tax Strategies for Investors."

The goal of this book is to get you to a place where you actually have a tax problem because of all the money, your money, is making for you. In retirement there are several strategies that will help you lower your tax burden, but while you are still working your salary determines your costs. You owe what you owe depending on deductions and on taxable income.

CHAPTER 15

RETIREMENT STRATEGIES

"If you want to be financially-free, you need to become a different person than you are today and let go of whatever has held you back in the past."
– Kim Kiyosaki, entrepreneur and author

"And from the age of fifty years they shall cease waiting upon the service thereof, and shall serve no more:" Numbers 8:25

As I interview retirees who understand the stock market, and certain financial planners I find they tend to over-use the word "conservative" as it relates to retirement. The primary goal in retirement is to have enough money to maintain a certain lifestyle without out-living your money. In other words, you don't want to live longer than your money is available (at a certain yearly income). What's good about getting older is the tenancy to spend less, but that is usually offset by increases in medical bills. As we age, we tend to have more visits to the doctor, more medications, and more aches and pains. Let me suggest you begin now with a consistent exercise routine of walking, water aerobics, and stretching to lessen the effects of age. Not only will you feel better, but your money will last longer as well.

For those jobs that offer Retirement Health Accounts (RHA), it is imperative to make sure you do everything possible to fund this account. Most employers will put money into this account every month based on the number of hours you worked. My employer for instance, puts $1.00 into my RHA account for every hour that I work, and all the money in excess of the employer maximum yearly contribution to my 401K, will help fund my RHA. The best part of the RHA is the triple tax break you get on the money. The money that goes in is pre-tax, it grows tax-free, and eventually you can spend it tax free for eligible medical expenses.

Find out from your employer if you have an RHA, and if so, what your options are for contributing to it.

So, what does it mean to be "conservative" after retirement? It means you can accept little to no losses to your principal balance of retirement funds. Many planners suggest fixed income assets such as bonds, T-Bills, and municipal bonds. These assets will allow you to keep your principal safe and use the proceeds of the interest for living expenses. For instance, if you have $1 million in bonds that pay an average of 5 percent, twice a year you will receive an interest payment of $25,000 for a total of $50,000. If you add in social security benefits your gross monthly income will be $6900.00 on average, or $83,600.00 per year. The problem will be to find government backed guaranteed bonds that pay greater than 3-4 percent.

Another solution could be considered less conservative, and that is a combination of bonds, along with stocks that pay dividends in the 3-6 percent range. These would have to be blue-chip companies with a solid past and future. A few household names come to mind, but you should get advice from your financial planner to choose those companies.

Another strategy to boost your retirement income is to delay your social security benefits. Your benefit increases approximately 8 percent a year for each year you delay up to age 70. For instance, the max social security benefit occurs at age 66 and a half ($2861), but if you delay till age 70 your gross amount increases to $3662. If you are still working and don't need to draw social security early, and you typically don't average greater than 8% annual returns on your investments, this seems like a safe option to increase your income in retirement.

However, if you have been averaging greater than 8 percent per year from your investments, you may want to discuss taking your social security earlier and investing these funds. (Ask your financial planner how your account has performed to make this decision.) If your returns have been steady and your investment advisor (IA) estimates it will continue to do so, you may consider being more aggressive while you are still working and put these funds to work at 10-12 percent per year. From 2008-2018 the NASDQ average return was just north of 15 percent compounded annually (see chart below). These numbers are based on SPY (SPDR S&P 500 ETF) from the end of 2008 until August 2, 2019.

Original Investment 69

Investment Return   287

Term   10   Years   0   Months

Or select investment period

From   From Date   to   To Date

Reset   Calculate

Gain or Loss: **218.00**
Return on Investment: **315.94%**
Simple Annualized ROI: **31.59%**
Compound Annual ROI: **15.32%**
Investment Period: **10 yr 0 mo**

In this example a $69 investment grew to $285 over a 10-year period. If we apply that same logic and interest rate to a monthly investment of $2861 beginning at 66.5 years of age until age 70, you will acquire ~$162,574.36 (see chart below). This will allow you to invest the funds you receive at 15.32 percent for the next 3 and a half years.

< Home   **TVM Calculator** Advanced   ?

Present Value **-2,861**   PV

Payment **-2,861**   PMT

Future Value **162,574.36**   FV

Annual Rate% **15.32**   Rate

Periods **42**   Periods

Compounding   Monthly

This is a great way to still contribute to your overall portfolio until you have to honor the required minimum distribution requirements at age 70.5. Retirement can be a lot of things, but it should not be boring, and you should not be poor.

Here is a list of retirement tax strategies to help you navigate where to pull money from and deciding which pot of money is more expensive than the others. It's important to get an expert in the area of retirement who can help you navigate the murky waters of taxes and retirement. This was taken from an article written by Kevin Webb, a CFP with Kehoe Financial Advisors as it appeared in Kiplinger.com on January 28, 2019.

1. Zero Percent Capital Gains

When you stop taking a salary, you're more likely to be eligible to pay zero taxes on your long-term capital gains. Low-income taxpayers (individuals with taxable incomes below $39,375 and couples filing jointly with taxable incomes below $78,750 in 2019) are eligible for this 0% long-term capital gains rate.

With advanced planning, even with significant assets you can intentionally find yourself in the lower brackets for the first couple years of retirement and take advantage of the zero percent long-term capital gains tax. For instance, you can delay taking Social Security for a couple years while you live off your zero percent capital gains. If you need more income, money withdrawn from a Roth IRA would not increase taxable income or affect the zero percent tax rate on the capital gain withdrawal.

To see how this could save you a lot of money, consider a couple with a $250,000 investment account with a $100,000 long-term capital gain. In most cases, this gain would result in $15,000 in taxes. But if the couple delay Social Security for a year and have no other taxable income, they can liquidate the $250,000 account and pay nothing on the $100,000 gain, saving them $15,000 in taxes. (Their income of $100,000 would be reduced by the 2019 standard deduction of $24,400, giving them taxable income of $75,600, under the $78,750 limit). Any of the $250,000 not needed for expenses can be used to purchase the exact same investments at a now-higher cost basis. (Webb, 2019)

2. Qualified Charitable Contributions (QCD)

You can make a QCD to your favorite charity after you have gained the age of 70.5 years old. It will help defer some taxes so the amount of the QCD will lower your taxable amount dollar for dollar.

With a QCD, make a charitable contribution up to $100,000 from your pre-tax IRA and the amount is excluded from your income. Not only are you able to take the standard deduction, you have effectively added the charitable deduction on top of that. Plus, a QCD counts toward satisfying your required minimum distribution. (Webb, 2019)

3. Roth Conversion

I have included the tax brackets for the lower incomes below, but this strategy is a great way to significantly reduce your tax burden.

If you own a traditional IRA, and are able to keep taxable income low, you may want to consider a Roth IRA conversion. While it's true that each dollar you convert will add to your taxable income, paying that tax now may result in less taxes paid overall. Also, money in a Roth is not subject to required minimum distributions at age 70.5.

One trick with Roth IRA conversions is to do a partial conversion in an amount that takes you to the top of your current tax bracket. So, if you are in the 12% tax bracket, convert enough of the traditional IRA into the Roth to stay in that bracket without moving up to the next one. Doing this over a few years can substantially reduce your overall tax burden moving forward. (Webb, 2019)

Tax Bracket Filing Status	Single	Married Filing Jointly or Qualifying Widow
10%	$0 to $9,700	$0 to $19,400
12%	$9,701 to $39,475	$19,401 to $78,950
22%	$39,476 to $84,200	$78,951 to $168,400
24%	$84,201 to $160,725	$168,401 to $321,450
32%	$160,726 to $204,100	$321,451 to $408,200
35%	$204,101 to $510,300	$408,201 to $612,350
37%	$510,301 or more	$612,351 or more

Tax Bracket Filing Status	Married Filing Separately	Head of Household
10%	$0 to $9,700	$0 to $13,850
12%	$9,701 to $39,475	$13,851 to $52,850
22%	$39,476 to $84,200	$52,851 to $84,200
24%	$84,201 to $160,725	$84,201 to $160,700
32%	$160,726 to $204,100	$160,701 to $204,100
35%	$204,101 to $306,175	$204,101 to $510,300
37%	$306,176 or more	$510,301 or more

(Rose, 2018)

4. Net Unrealized Appreciation

This is a great strategy to help save on taxes in retirement if you have company stock. If you are retiring with a 401(k) plan that has company stock in it, you may have an important decision to make that will affect future taxes. If you qualify and follow IRS guidelines, you may be able to take advantage of special tax treatment for the net unrealized appreciation (NUA) of the company stock. NUA is the difference between the company's current stock price and the amount you paid for it.

A common approach to 401(k) distributions is to roll the 401(k) over to an IRA, where withdrawals are taxed at your ordinary income level. With NUA treatment, the gain in the company stock is taxed at more favorable capital gains rates when sold, with only the cost basis portion being taxed as ordinary income rates. If the NUA makes up most of the account value with a minimal cost basis, this can result in significant tax savings. (Webb, 2019)

5. Strategic Investment Withdrawals

Investment accounts can be separated into three tax categories: taxable accounts (investments), tax-deferred accounts (traditional IRAs and 401(k)s), and tax-exempt accounts (Roth IRAs). Conventional wisdom is to withdraw first from taxable accounts, then tax-deferred accounts, while leaving tax-exempt accounts last. This allows the tax-advantaged accounts to continue growing. But this might be too simple of a solution.

A better idea is to take strategic withdrawals from whichever account best suits your taxable situation each year. One example is to tap the tax-deferred accounts in the early years of retirement to avoid large future required minimum distributions that push you into higher tax brackets. There are many other examples, too, but the idea is to have money in accounts that are taxed differently, allowing you to strategically tap them to minimize taxes through your retirement. This tax diversification also is helpful in responding to any future tax law changes. (Webb, 2019)

Remember there are fiduciaries that are available to help you and keep your interest first as your money begins to work for you, and you decide if you need or want help.

CHAPTER 16

ESTATE PLANNING!

"I believe that through knowledge and discipline, financial peace is possible for all of us." – **Dave Ramsey, personal finance guru, businessman, and author**

"House and riches are the inheritance of fathers:"
Proverbs 19:14

a. What's In An Estate Plan

Most people in the United States will not have an estate plan due to the lack of significant financial resources and literacy. It is still important to understand what it is, and how to make sure you are prepared if you need one. The following is reprinted from Investopedia and the explanation is a great start to begin gaining knowledge and understanding.

Estate planning involves planning for how an individual's assets will be preserved, managed, and distributed after death. It also takes into account the management of an individual's properties and financial obligations in the event that they become incapacitated. Assets that could make up an individual's estate include houses, cars, stocks, paintings, life insurance, pensions, and debt. Individuals have various reasons for planning an estate, such as preserving family wealth, providing for surviving spouse and children, funding children and/or grandchildren's education, or leaving their legacy behind to a charitable cause. (Kagan, Estate Planning: W, 2019)

b. Building Your Plan

The most basic step in estate planning involves writing a will. Other major estate planning tasks include:

- Limiting estate taxes by setting up trust accounts in the name of beneficiaries.

- Establishing a guardian for living dependents.

- Naming an executor of the estate to oversee the terms of the will.

- Creating/updating beneficiaries on plans such as life insurance, IRAs and 401(k)s.

- Setting up funeral arrangements.

- Establishing annual gifting to qualified charitable and non-profit organizations to reduce the taxable estate.

- Setting up durable power of attorney (POA) to direct other assets and investments.

(Kagan, Estate Planning: W, 2019)

The discussions for planning your estate should start as soon as you realize you may have some assets that have to be dealt with in case you are incapacitated or God forbid, dead. Either way getting a retirement expert and or estate planner to help you is an excellent use of your money. If you start early, no later than 40-45 years old, your provider will be able to manipulate the plan to grow and expand as you acquire more resources.

CHAPTER 17

FINANCIAL FREEDOM -"FINALLY"

"You become financially free when your passive income exceeds your expenses." – T. Harv Eker, author, businessman and motivational speaker

"Stand fast therefore in the liberty wherewith Christ hath made us free, and be not entangled again with the yoke of bondage." Galatians 5:1

a. True Financial Freedom

"Being able to live life without financial worries!" But, don't be fooled money is not the only answer:

> Just because you have money does not mean you have financial freedom. In my book, It's Rising Time, I talk about how people like Ed McMahon from The Tonight Show and Nicole Murphy, the ex-wife of actor Eddie Murphy, had millions of dollars and lost it all. Nicole Murphy spent her $15-million divorce settlement in less than four

years. And toward the end of his life, Ed McMahon faced foreclosure on his Beverly Hills home and owed $747,000 in credit-card debt.

Both of these examples illustrate that even if you have a lot of money, if you don't know what to do with it, it will be gone.

Of course, it's also important to note that money isn't the thing that makes you truly rich — it's the freedom that comes from pursuing whatever brings you joy and provides you with fulfillment that makes you rich. The whole point of financial freedom is that once you become financially free, you have more choices of how to live your life and spend your days. (Kiyosaki K. , 2019)

Randall Rochon, a pilot with United Airlines states his definition of financial freedom is: "To have enough financial resources to cover daily expenses in perpetuity without stress!"

John Brennan says it means "Having no debt including your home. Also having enough money to retire and be able to reach 90 years old without any worries. It includes enough money for anticipated medical expenses without breaking the bank…you have to have enough money to give your children and your children's children a head start."

I know some people want to say it depends on your status, spending habits, and other personality traits. It really has to do with your passive income covering your daily expenses, and any unforeseen emergencies. But how important is it. Some people will go through their entire lives never knowing the reduced stress, balanced life, and philanthropic blessings of being financially free. Hopefully this book will give you a taste of what it truly means to live with no debt, having the ability to help others without a second thought, being able to slow down and think of ways to improve all of mankind and not just your own status in life, and finally, being able to leave a legacy to the generations to come.

b. You Have To Define Financial Freedom For Yourself

If you like expensive things, you may not be able to continue those type of purchases once in retirement. On the other hand, if your tastes change, you may have more than you need, especially if you downsize your living expenses! It is important to know what will give you a sense of freedom. Some people want to be able to get away from it all and retire to a tropical island. Others want to see and experience the world. Still others just want to be around family and friends and experience what comes with living a quiet existence. Personally, I want to be able to influence the minds of people in order to end hatred, strife, bitterness, bigotry, homelessness, illiteracy, and all the other ills of our society. Frederick Douglas, Martin Luther King, Jr., and other dynamic leaders have touted "We are not free until we are all free." We have to help each other become better fathers, mothers, sons, daughters, people, friends, and citizens.

It seems lofty, but this is my why! This is why I am writing this book. This is why I share the information for free for anyone who will listen. We can make a difference and together we will be victorious.

CHAPTER 18

ESTABLISHING LEGACY

"A good financial plan is a road map that shows us exactly how the choices we make today will affect our future."
– Alexa Von Tobel, founder and CEO of LearnVest.com

"A good man leaveth an inheritance to his children's children: and the wealth of the sinner is laid up for the just."
Proverbs 13:22

The bible says a man should leave an inheritance for his children. What's interesting is a man automatically leaves the inheritance, but sometimes it's not a great thing! So, one way or another your residue is what your children inherit. if it's good, pat yourself on the back, but if it's not good, you need to re-evaluate your why!

In our present culture, financial literacy seems to be reserved for only a few. All the changes in our grandparent's pension funds, getting paid until you die, those are a thing of the past. When I speak to young people most tell me they know about their company's 401K, but they don't have enough money to contribute to it. Many of them say

they won't be in the job long enough to benefit from contributing to the plan. As sad as this may seem to those who
understand time value of money, it's all too common among
the majority of Americans. This phenomenon is not limited
by color, socio-economic background, or education (finance
majors withstanding). I work with highly intelligent people
who understand the importance of savings, living below their
means, starting out of debt, and protecting a great credit score.
But if I ask them about their investments, many times their
eyes glaze over and they say I guess it's doing ok. The problem is with our educational system which doesn't encourage
financial literacy.

In the past, the company that you worked for took care
of you financially, after giving them 30-40 years of service,
through pension plans and large severance packages, or
through government retirement plans. Today's plans include
the 401K, 401B, KEOGH plans, IRAs, and golden parachutes
for those at the top. Not many personal plans exist unless you
count the government plans, TSPs and other retirement vehicles used by the armed forces and other government branches.

That being said, legacy is something you do, for others, not
for yourself. It's a way to give to future generations whether to
your own children, or to the culture. The bible says we should
teach our children from the time we get up until we lay down
at night. Since it's hard to teach what we don't know, usually
children learn through what they see modeled by adults in their
lives. Whether good or bad, what they see is what they get. Most
shows my children watch show young adults flaunting expensive cars, jewelry, clothes, and exotic vacations. They then talk
as though they can just snap their fingers and by magic these
things appear. Although my wife and I have tried to explain
how unrealistic this is, they continue to pursue careers in areas
that may not give them what they see!

So, we teach them by example. We buy dependable but used vehicles with great track records. We save, stay out of debt, and invest on a monthly basis. We share with them the benefits of planning ahead and show them the power of compound interest. As we go through the numbers with them, their eyes glaze over until we mention what they will have at retirement age. They perk up and ask that infamous question, "Why can't we spend some of that money now?"

The bible clearly lays out the plan for investing; seed, time, harvest. If you eat your seed, time won't matter, because you will never have a harvest. But if you use some of your seed, plant it, take care of it, and watch it grow; over time, you will reap a harvest. After explaining this, the children seem to accept they have to wait a while before they start spending the millions of dollars they may see in retirement. In the meantime, they grumble and ask, "So when can we start spending it?"

We decided to start investment accounts for each child at $100-200.00 per month (at the time, our children were nine and ten years old). We invested in companies they liked such as Nike, Apple, Visa, and Starbucks. If you have been following either of these companies for the past twenty years, you will see the returns are much greater than the overall market and especially what the so-called experts tell you to expect (6-8 percent). Take our grandson for instance, we encouraged our daughter and her husband to start his investment account as soon as he had a social security number. Today, he is three years old with a net worth greater than $10,000. All of his grandparents are contributing $50 per month and his parents $50 each, for a total of $250 per month. If this investment continues for sixty-five years with an annual return (before tax) of 12 percent, it will grow to $191K by the time he's eighteen, and $59 million by age sixty-five.

What if you only could invest $50 total per month, and the parents along with the grandparents helped at $10 per month. Even with these small amounts the totals would be: $38K at 18 years old and $11 million at the age of 65. How about that for creating a legacy. The problem will be making it happen. First you have to be disciplined, then you have to be brave when others are afraid. Thirdly, you have to never quit, even when those all around you quit, and finally you have to be consistently committed to your goal. One of the main things that made me continue in spite of having to start over twice, was reading about how the experts did it.

Gurus like Warren Buffett, Peter Lynch, Robert Kiyosaki, and Tony Robins taught me a very valuable lesson, "twice". They taught that you first have to have a plan. You have to give the plan time to work by being committed and consistent, and after a period of time you have to evaluate the plan. You may have to consider your implementation of the plan, in other words, did you follow the plan? If you followed the plan and the results of your labor were below overall market performance, you should consider revising your plan or switch to a broad market investment strategy. At the end of the day you have to hold yourself accountable, and if you have a financial advisor, you have to hold them accountable. Plans will and always will be somewhat flexible, but if it always changes based on your gut or your mood, then you don't really have a plan. At that point, you just have thoughts!

1. Have/make a plan.
2. Be consistent and committed.
3. Give the plan time to work.
4. Re-evaluate the plan.
5. Make small changes and refer to step two.
6. Teach the plan to your children.

In the end, you and your family will be better off by trying to take care of the money that you count on, taking care
of you.

Lastly, you should think about putting everything of value
on a trust fund for your children. Trusts can be very useful,
when you are trying to build wealth and protecting it from
overly aggressive tax laws.

CHAPTER 19

CONCLUSION

"There is a secret psychology of money. Most people don't know about it. That's why most people never become financially successful. A lack of money is not the problem; it is merely a symptom of what's going on inside of you."
– T. Harv Eker, author, businessman and motivational speaker

"And thus shall ye say to him that liveth in prosperity, Peace be both to thee, and peace be to thine house, and peace be unto all that thou hast." 1 Samuel 25:6

It has been a labor of love for me to pen this book. I have had a lot of help from a lot of sources, but mostly life! It teaches you lessons that sometimes books cannot, and in ways that you will never forget. I have tried to re-create the circumstances surrounding my financial woes and issues and give an inside perspective of how devastating a lack of financial literacy can be. On the other hand, the pure joy of knowing there is a way back from the brink of financial disaster makes me smile.

I reprinted this from a Market Watch article 11/19/2018:

Can you guess who's been loading up on stocks at a faster pace than anyone during the past 30 years? It's not Wall Street titans and kajillionaires on the Forbes richest lists. It's mid- to lower-income households, particularly those pulling in less than $42,000 a year.

In the late 1980s, fewer than one-third of Americans owned equities. Fast forward to 2016 and, according to Federal Reserve Board data, that number shot up to more than half (52%) of U.S. households. (Go us!)

Even better, it's not just wealthy households adding equities to their already brimming coffers: It's households on the lowest rungs of the income ladder (those making less than $24,000 annually and between $24,000 and $42,000) participating in the great wealth-building machine that is the stock market. Stock ownership more than doubled for these households between 1989 and 2016, according to Investment Company Institute tabulations of the Fed data.

All told, today nearly 4 out of 10 households that invest in stocks make less than $68,000 a year.

How Did That Happen?

What's changed since 1989? Access changed! Specifically, access to workplace retirement savings plans, like 401(k)s, and personal investment accounts, like IRAs. Quirky Super Bowl ads for discount brokers and job listings touting the employer match on 401(k) contributions are relatively new developments: 401(k) plans and IRAs were just starting to take off in the '80s. And the Roth IRA didn't come along until 1997.

Thanks to tax incentives (contributions to these accounts can dramatically lower what you owe the IRS) and the death of company pension plans, money flooded into the market.

Today, the ICI estimates that there is more than $5 trillion in 401(k) plans and more than $9 trillion in individual retirement accounts — and that half or more of the dollars in those plans is invested in stocks.

Jump On The Bandwagon

If retirement, or some other version of financial freedom, is on your radar, stocks should be, too. Cash simply won't cut it for long-term savings.

Over time inflation causes cash to lose its potency, or how much a wad of it can purchase. You can see how much sitting on the sidelines will cost you in potential earnings over time by using a cost of cash calculator.

If dabbling in individual stocks sounds like something you want to try, start small, slow and even consider using fake money at first via a stock market simulator. Some online brokers offer potential customers free access to their virtual trading platforms to take a test drive without risking your lunch money. The fewer investments you have in your portfolio, the greater your exposure to risk.

Regardless of the investing strategy you choose, and no matter where you fall on the income scale, stock ownership should be a part of your long-term investing strategy.

Opinion: Forget the fiduciary standard — financial advisers need a code of ethics

Published: May 24, 2017 9:12 a.m. ET6

Financial advisers should be like doctors and take a 'Hippocratic oath'

By MICHAEL EDESESS

Doctors take an oath to do no harm to your health, but financial advisers don't have to take a similar one to do no harm to your portfolio.

The U.S. Department of Labor's proposed Fiduciary Rule, which would require advisers to act in their customers' best interests, will begin to take effect June 9. But why is a rule to prevent financial advisers from hurting their clients' finances even needed?

It could be argued that such a 1,023 page piece of legislation should not be necessary, if only advisers were already bound by a strong ethical commitment.

If they were, they would feel obliged to know when their advice to clients may be worse than other advice they could offer — and to refrain from giving the inferior advice, even if it hurts their own wallets.

The Hippocratic oath taken by doctors is a strong ethical commitment, and operates as if it had the force of law. No such strong ethical commitment is made by most financial advisers.

In fact, many advisers offer harmful financial products because they make the advisers a lot of money.

Gary Cohn, Trump's chief economic adviser, has even said that a knock on the fiduciary rule is that it would be "Like putting only healthy food on the menu."

Suppose we were to apply Cohn's quote to doctors instead of financial advisers: Should doctors be allowed to prescribe medicines that are harmful to their clients' health but lucrative for themselves?

When financial advisers give bad advice, it's partly because the "science" of financial advice is nowhere near as clear as the science of medicine. But it is also because often the more money an investment adviser or manager earns on a product or service, the less the customer earns.

And many advisers are afraid to recommend that you do nothing when that is the appropriate recommendation, as it very often is, because they think you'll realize you don't need them. So they sometimes recommend action at your expense and usually their gain, when lack of action would be better.

Vetting a financial adviser

How can you tell if a financial adviser will help and won't harm your finances?

First, the adviser will tell you upfront that they're not going to be able to help you beat the stock market.

They will make their fees crystal clear and tell you each year exactly what fees they are being paid in dollars and for what purpose.

Such an adviser will probably charge by the hour, for specific tasks that they are asked to do — or perhaps just for an annual or biennial "checkup," like a doctor does, if the customer asks for it.

A good financial adviser will not be wealthy, unless he or she had an inheritance, or previously made a killing in a Silicon Valley startup, or has simply been very frugal and saving for a long time — because otherwise, if a financial adviser is very wealthy it means the adviser got the money from his or her customers, which means the customers now have less.

How can financial advisers prove that they have their clients' best interests in mind?

They will need to do what doctors have done. They will need to have a strict code of ethics and adhere to it, and diligently root out others who do not adhere.

As part of their code of ethics, they will need to

strictly refrain from recommending any product or action to their clients if they don't know whether it is as likely to be harmful as beneficial.

If they cannot do these things then they cannot call themselves financial advisers. And the community of financial advisers, which should be an ethical community, should drum them out of their community.

Unethical advisers who sell bad products, purportedly without knowing they are bad, bring to mind Upton Sinclair's now-famous saying, "It is hard to get a man to understand something if his salary depends on his not understanding it."

*Economist and mathematician Michael Edesess is chief investment strategist of Compendium Finance, adviser to mobile financial planning software company **Plynty**, and a research associate of the **Edhec-Risk Institute**. E-mail him at **michael.edesess@gmail.com**. Follow him on Twitter at **@MichaelEdesess**.* (Edesess, 2017)

FINANCIAL QUOTES

*"You don't have to work as hard,
if your money is working harder!"*

"Buy equities on sale!"

Those by Warren Buffett—

1. "What we learn from history is that people don't learn from history."

2. "Long ago, Ben Graham taught me that 'Price is what you pay; value is what you get. Whether we're talking about socks or stocks, I like buying quality merchandise when it is marked down."

3. "Successful investing takes time, discipline and patience. No matter how great the talent or effort, some things just take time: You can't produce a baby in one month by getting nine women pregnant."

4. "Diversification is a protection against ignorance. It makes very little sense for those who know what they're doing."

5. "If you aren't willing to own a stock for ten years, don't even think about owning it for ten minutes. Put together a portfolio of companies whose aggregate earnings march upward over the years, and so also will the portfolio's market value."

6. "It's far better to buy a wonderful company at a fair price than a fair company at a wonderful price."

7. "The key to investing is not assessing how much an industry is going to affect society, or how much it will grow, but rather determining the competitive advantage of any given company and, above all, the durability of that advantage."

8. "I will tell you how to become rich. Close the doors. Be fearful when others are greedy. Be greedy when others are fearful."

9. "Rule No. 1 is never lose money. Rule No. 2 is never forget Rule No. 1."

10. "Widespread fear is your friend as an investor because it serves up bargain purchases."

11. "The best thing that happens to us is when a great company gets into temporary trouble... We want to buy them when they're on the operating table."

12. "Do not take yearly results too seriously. Instead, focus on four or five-year averages."

13. "Someone's sitting in the shade today because someone planted a tree a long time ago."

(Matthew Frankel, 2019)

GLOSSARY OF FINANCIAL TERMS

(Reprinted from Nationwide.com)

When reading about insurance and financial products, you may encounter financial terminology and acronyms that you aren't familiar with. These definitions are for informational and educational purposes only. Please discuss your specific situation or questions with an investment professional.

Active Management

The trading of securities to take advantage of market opportunities. In contrast to passive management, active managers rely on research, market forecasts, and their own judgment and experience in selecting securities to buy and sell.

Actuary

A mathematician who calculates premiums, reserves, dividends, insurance, pension and annuity rates for insurance and financial services companies.

Aggressive growth fund

An investment fund that takes higher risk of loss in return for potentially higher returns or gains.

Alpha

A measure of the difference between a fund's actual returns and its expected performance, given its level of risk as measured by beta. A positive alpha figure indicates the fund has performed better than its beta would predict. In contrast, a negative alpha indicates the fund's underperformance, given the expectations established by the fund's beta. Alpha, beta and R-squared are considered MPT (Modern Portfolio Theory) statistics and are based on a least-squared regression of the fund's return over Treasury bills (called excess return) and the excess returns of the fund's benchmark index.

Annual rate of return

The annual rate of gain or loss on an investment, expressed as a percentage.

Annual report

A yearly report or record of the financial position and operations of an investment or company.

Annuitant

The person whose life is insured is the annuitant. The annuitant and the annuity owner aren't necessarily the same person.

Annuitization

The time you spend contributing to your annuity is the accumulation phase. The annuitization phase begins when you start receiving money from your annuity.

Annuity

An insurance contract issued by a life insurance company. The contract provides income at regular intervals for a defined period of time, such as a specific number of years or for life.

Annuity commencement date

The date stated in the annuity contract indicating when annuity payments will begin. This is also known as the annuity start date.

Appreciation

An increase in the value of an investment.

Asset

Anything with commercial or exchange value that is owned by a business, institution or individual. Examples include cash, real estate and investments.

Asset allocation

Spreading your investments between asset categories (stocks, bonds, cash or cash equivalents) may help minimize risk. That's because investment categories respond to changing economic and political conditions in different ways. Just keep in mind that the use of asset allocation does not guarantee returns or insulate you from potential losses.

Asset class

A group of securities or investments that have similar characteristics and behave similarly in the marketplace. Three common asset classes are equities (such as stocks), fixed income (such as bonds), and cash alternatives or equivalents (such as money market accounts).

Asset-based fees

Expenses that are based on the amount of assets in your plan. These fees are generally charged as percentages or basis points.

Automatic asset rebalancing (AAR)

An optional service that will periodically exchange money between funds in your account to maintain your original investment levels. AAR saves you the time and hassle of manually reallocating your current balance every few months.

Average annual total returns

The annual compounded returns that would have produced the cumulative total return if fund performance had been constant during a given period.

Back-end load

A fee imposed by some funds when shares are redeemed (sold back to the fund) during the first few years of ownership. This is also referred to as a contingent deferred sales charge.

Balanced fund

A fund with an investment objective of both long-term growth and income, through investment in both stocks and bonds.

Basis point

One-hundredth of one percent, or 0.01%. For example, 20 basis points equals 0.20%. Investment expenses, interest rates, and yield differences among bonds are often expressed in basis points.

Benchmark

An unmanaged group of securities whose performance is used as a standard to measure investment performance. Some well-known benchmarks are the Dow Jones Industrial Average and the S&P 500 Index.

Beta

A measure of a fund's sensitivity to market movements. The beta of the market is 1.00 by definition. Morningstar calculates beta by comparing a fund's excess return over Treasury bills to the market's excess return over Treasury bills. A beta of 1.10 shows that the fund has performed 10% better than its benchmark index in up markets and 10% worse in down markets, assuming all other factors remain constant. Conversely, whereas a beta of 0.85 indicates that the fund's excess return is expected to perform 15% worse than the market's excess return during up markets and 15% better during down markets. Alpha, beta and R-squared are considered MPT (Modern Portfolio Theory) statistics and are based on a least-squared regression of the fund's return over Treasury bills (called excess return) and the excess returns of the fund's benchmark index.

Bond

A debt security that represents money borrowed by a corporation, government, or other entity. The borrower repays the amount of the loan, plus a percentage as interest. Income funds generally invest in bonds.

Bond fund

A fund that invests primarily in bonds and other debt instruments.

Bond rating

A rating or grade that's intended to indicate the credit quality of a bond. The financial strength of its issuer and the likelihood that it will repay the debt are considered. Agencies such as Standard & Poor's, Moody's Investors Service and Fitch issue ratings for different bonds, ranging from AAA (highly unlikely to default) to D (in default).

Broker

A person who acts as an intermediary between the buyer and seller of a security, insurance product or mutual fund. This person is often paid a commission. The terms broker, broker/dealer and dealer are sometimes used interchangeably.

Brokerage window

An optional service lets you establish a self-directed brokerage account. This option carries distinct charges.

Capital appreciation fund

An investment fund that seeks growth in share prices by investing primarily in stocks whose share prices are expected to rise.

Capital gain

An increase in the value of an investment, calculated by the difference between the net purchase price and the net sales price.

Capital loss

The loss in the value of an investment, calculated by the difference between the purchase price and the net sales price.

Capital preservation

An investment goal or objective to keep the original investment amount (the principal) from decreasing in value.

Capitalization (Cap)

The total market value of a company's outstanding equity.

Cash alternative / cash equivalent

An investment that is short term, highly liquid, and has high credit quality.

Cash refund annuity

An annuity that makes periodic payments during your lifetime, as well as a benefit to your beneficiaries upon your death. Your death benefit is equal to your premium(s) paid; minus payments made during your lifetime.

Class A shares

Class A shares typically impose a front-end sales load and tend to have a lower 12b-1 fee and lower annual expense than other mutual fund share classes. Some mutual funds reduce the front-end load as the size of the investment increases.

Collective investment fund (CIF)

Investments created by a bank or trust company for employee benefit plans, such as 401(k) plans. Also referred to as collective or commingled trusts, CIFs pool the assets of retirement plans for investment purposes. CIFs are governed by rules and regulations that apply to banks and trust companies instead of being registered with the SEC.

Commission

Compensation paid to a broker or other salesperson when investments are bought or sold.

Common stock

An investment that represents a share of ownership in a corporation.

Company stock fund

A fund that invests primarily in employer securities that may also maintain a cash position for liquidity purposes.

Compounding

The cumulative effect that reinvesting an investment's earnings can have by generating additional earnings of their own.

Contract issue date

The date you sign paperwork to buy an annuity.

Corporate bond

A bond issued by a corporation, rather than by a government. The credit risk for a corporate bond is based on the repayment ability of the company that issued the bond.

Credit risk

The risk that a bond issuer will default. In other words, not repay principal or interest to the investor, as promised. This is also known as default risk.

Current yield

The current rate of return of an investment. This is calculated by dividing the investment's expected income payments by its current market price.

Custodian

A person or entity, such as a bank or trust company, responsible for holding financial assets.

Deferred annuity

A deferred annuity lets you potentially grow your assets so

they could provide a steady stream of income during retirement. When you purchase the annuity, you deposit money into it over a period of time. That money is invested. At a certain point, usually at retirement, you start receiving payments from the annuity. These payments can be made in a lump sum or in installments.

Deflation

The opposite of inflation, deflation is a decline in the prices of goods and services.

Depreciation

A decrease in the value of an investment.

Designated investment alternative

Your plan's investment options.

Distribution

Money you take from your financial account, such as an IRA. Also called a withdrawal.

Diversification

The practice of investing in multiple asset classes and securities with different risk characteristics.

Dividend

Money an investment fund or company pays to its stockholders, typically from profits. The amount is usually expressed on a per-share basis.

Duration

An estimate of bond price sensitivity to changes in interest rates. The higher the duration, the greater the change (higher risk) in relation to interest-rate movements.

Earnings

Money gained on the principal in your financial accounts, such as an IRA.

Emerging market

Generally, economies that are in the process of growth and industrialization. Developing markets, such as Africa, Asia, Eastern Europe, the Far East, Latin America and the Middle East may hold significant growth potential in the future. Investing in emerging markets may provide significant rewards, as well as significant risks.

Emerging market fund

A fund that invests primarily in emerging market countries.

Employee Retirement Income Security Act of 1974 (ERISA)

A federal law that imposes various requirements on voluntary established pension plans in the private industry. ERISA establishes standards in order to provide protection for plan participants.

Equity

A security or investment representing ownership in a corporation. Equity is often used interchangeably with stock. Compare to a bond, which represents a loan to a borrower.

Equity Fund

A fund that invests primarily in equities.

Exchange traded fund (ETF)

An investment company, such as a mutual fund. ETF shares are traded throughout the day on stock exchanges at market-determined prices.

Expense ratio

A measure of what it costs to operate an investment, expressed as a percentage of its assets or in basis points. You pay for these costs through a reduction in the investment's rate of return. See operating expenses and total annual operating expenses.

Federal Deposit Insurance Corporation (FDIC)

A federal agency that insures deposits in member banks and thrift institutions.

Fiduciary

Any person or party who exercises any discretionary authority or control over the management of a plan, or the disposition of its assets. For a fee, a fiduciary gives investment advice, or has the authority to do so. A fiduciary also has discretionary responsibility in the administration of that plan.

Financial Industry Regulatory Authority (FINRA)

A self-regulatory organization for brokerage firms doing business in the United States. FINRA operates under the supervision of the U.S. Securities and Exchange Commission (SEC). FINRA protects investors and ensures market integrity.

Financial statement

The written record of the financial status of a fund or company. Financial statements are usually published in a company's annual report. They generally include a balance sheet, an income statement, and other financial statements and disclosures.

Fixed annuity

With a fixed annuity, the insurance company guarantees the rate of return and payout. Guarantees are subject to the claims-paying ability of the issuing insurance company.

Fixed income fund

A fund that invests primarily in bonds and other fixed-income securities. Fixed income funds often provide shareholders with current income.

Fixed return investment

An investment that provides a specific rate of return to the investor.

Flat rate expenses

Base fees charged to a plan, regardless of the number of participants. Examples of flat rate expenses include preparation of IRS Form 5500, discrimination testing and vesting calculation.

Front-end load

A sales charge on mutual funds or annuities assessed at the time of purchase.

Fund family

A group or "complex" of mutual funds. Each group typically has its own investment objective and is managed and distributed by the same company. Fund family also refers to a group of collective investment funds or a group of separate accounts managed and distributed by the same company.

Fund window

A plan feature that lets you buy investments that are not included in your plan's general menu of designated investment alternatives.

Global fund

A fund that invests primarily in securities anywhere in the world, including the United States.

Government securities

Any debt obligations issued by a government or its agencies, such as U.S. Treasury bills.

Group annuity contract

An annuity contract between an insurance company and an owner for the benefit of a designated group, such as retirement plan participants.

Growth and income fund

A fund that has a dual strategy of growth or capital appreciation, as well as current income generation through dividends or interest payments.

Growth fund

A fund that invests primarily in the stocks of companies with above-average risk in return for potentially above-average gains. These companies often pay little or no dividends, and their stock prices tend to have the most ups and downs from day to day.

Guaranteed interest account

An account within a fixed or variable annuity that is guaranteed by the insurance company to earn at least a minimum rate of interest while invested in the contract.

Guaranteed investment contract

A contract issued by an insurance company that guarantees a specific rate of return on an investment over a certain time period.

Guaranteed lifetime withdrawal benefit

A feature sometimes offered in an annuity contract where the insurance company lets you withdraw a specified amount from an account. This benefit can apply to your entire life, the joint lives of you and another individual (such as your spouse) or for a specified period of time. Withdrawals can be made even if the account balance is reduced to zero. This benefit it also known as a guaranteed minimum withdrawal benefit.

Immediate annuity

You can convert a lump sum into payments for life or for a certain number of years from an immediate annuity. Payments begin immediately.

Inception date

The date a fund's operations begin.

Income fund

A fund that primarily seeks current income rather than capital appreciation.

Index

A benchmark used to evaluate a fund's performance. The most common indexes for stock funds are the Dow Jones Industrial Average and the Standard & Poor's 500 Index.

Index fund

An investment fund that seeks to parallel the performance of a particular stock market or bond market index. Often referred to as passively-managed investments.

Individual annuity contract

An annuity contract between an insurance company and a person or persons.

Individual Retirement Account (IRA)

IRAs are accounts that you own and fund through your own contributions. Two common types of IRAs are:

- **Traditional IRAs** – Contributions are made with pre-tax dollars, and earnings are tax-deferred. This means that you don't owe taxes until the funds are withdrawn, usually at retirement.

- **Roth IRAs** – Contributions are made with after-tax dollars, so you don't pay taxes on the money as it accumulates.

Individual service expenses

Charges applied to participants who take advantage of special plan features, such as participant loans.

Inflation

The general upward price movement of goods and services in an economy. Inflation is generally one of the major risks to investors over the long term because it erodes the purchasing power of their savings.

Interest / Interest rate

The fee charged by a lender to a borrower, usually expressed as an annual percentage of the principal. For example, someone investing in bonds will receive interest payments from the bond's issuer.

Interest rate risk

The possibility that the market value of a bond or bond fund will decrease due to rising interest rates. When interest rates (and bond yields) go up, bond prices usually go down, and vice versa.

International fund

A fund that invests primarily in the securities of companies located outside of the United States. Or whose revenues come from outside the United States.

Investment adviser

A person or organization hired by an investment fund or an individual to give professional advice on investments and asset management practices.

Investment company

A corporation or trust that invests pooled shareholder dollars in securities that are appropriate to the organization's objective. The most common type of investment company, a mutual fund, stands ready to buy back its shares at their current net asset value.

Investment objective

The goal that an investment fund or investor seeks to achieve, such as growth or income.

Investment return

The gain or loss on an investment over a certain period, expressed as a percentage. Income and capital gains or losses are included in calculating the investment return.

Investment risk

The possibility of losing some or all of the amounts invested, or not gaining value in an investment.

Joint and last survivor annuity

An annuity that provides periodic payments for the joint lives of two individuals. Benefits are payable upon the death of one individual to the surviving individual at a percentage of the original payment amount. Death benefit amounts depend on the terms of the contract.

Large capitalization (Cap)

A reference to either a large company stock or an investment fund that invests in the stocks of large companies.

Large-cap fund

A fund that invests primarily in large-cap stocks.

Large-cap stocks

Stocks of companies with a large market capitalization. Large caps tend to be well-established companies, so their stocks typically have less risk than smaller caps, but they also offer less potential for dramatic growth.

Life annuity

An annuity that makes periodic payments only for the life of one individual. Also known as a single life annuity.

Liquidity

The ease that an investment can be converted into cash. If a security is very liquid, it can be bought or sold easily. If a security is not liquid, it may take additional time and/or a lower price to sell it.

Longevity risk

The risk that you will live longer than expected and run out of retirement money.

Management fee

A service fee or charge paid to an investment manager.

Market capitalization (Cap)

The market value of a company. Market capitalization can be determined by multiplying the number of outstanding shares of a company's stock by the stock's current market price per share.

Market risk

The possibility that the value of an investment will fall because of a general decline in the financial markets.

Maturity date

The date when the principal amount of a loan, bond or any other debt becomes due and is to be paid in full.

Mid capitalization (Cap)

A reference to either a medium-sized company stock or an investment fund that invests in the stocks of medium-sized companies.

Mid-cap fund

A fund that invests primarily in mid-cap stocks.

Mid-cap stocks

Stocks of companies with a medium market capitalization. Mid-caps are often considered to offer more growth potential than larger caps, but less than small caps. They also are considered to offer less risk than small caps, but more than large caps.

Money market fund

A mutual fund that invests in short-term, high-grade fixed-income securities. Money market funds seek the highest level of income consistent with preserving capital. In other words, they try to maintain a stable share price.

Morningstar

A leading mutual fund research and tracking firm that categorizes funds by objective and size, then ranks fund performance within those categories.

Mutual fund

An investment company registered with the SEC that buys a portfolio of securities selected by a professional investment adviser. Mutual funds can have actively-managed portfolios, where a professional investment adviser creates a unique mix of investments to meet a particular investment objective. They can also have passively-managed portfolios, in which the adviser tries to match the performance of a selected benchmark or index.

NASDAQ-100 Index

An unmanaged index that includes 100 of the largest domestic and international nonfinancial securities listed on the Nasdaq Stock Market, based on market capitalization.

National Association of Securities Dealers Automated Quotation (NASDAQ)

A composite index that measures the performance of more than 5,000 U.S. and non-U.S. companies traded "over the counter" through NASDAQ.

Net asset value (NAV)

The net dollar value of a single investment fund share or unit that is calculated by the fund on a daily basis.

New York Stock Exchange (NYSE)

The oldest and largest stock exchange in the United States. The NYSE was founded in 1792.

No-load fund

A mutual fund whose shares are sold without a sales commission. No-load funds do not charge a combined 12b-1 fee and service fee of more than 25 basis points, or 0.25% per year.

Operating expenses

Costs associated with running or operating an investment fund. Operating expenses may include custody fees, management fees and transfer agent fees. Also see expense ratio and total annual operating expenses.

P/E ratio

The price of a stock divided by trailing 12-month earnings per share.

Passive management

The process or approach to operating or managing a fund in a passive or non-active manner, typically with the goal of mirroring an index. Passive management funds are often referred to as index funds and differ from investment funds that are actively managed.

Per participant charges

Charges are based on the total number of eligible employees or actual participants in the plan.

Period certain

A payment feature available in some annuity contracts that guarantees periodic payments for a set period of time. For example, in a life annuity, periodic payments would be made to you or beneficiary for the either the guaranteed period or the life of the individual. Whichever is longer.

Plan administrative expenses

Charges used to cover services provided for the day-to-day operations of the plan, such as recordkeeping, accounting, customer service support and daily valuation.

Portfolio

A collection of investments, such as stocks and bonds owned by an individual, organization or investment fund.

Portfolio manager

The individual, team or firm making the investment decisions for an investment fund, including the selection of individual investments.

Portfolio turnover rate

A measure of how frequently investments are bought and sold within an investment fund during a year. The portfolio turnover rate is usually expressed as a percentage of the total value of an investment fund.

Principal

Money you've contributed to your financial account, such as an IRA.

Prospectus

The official document that describes certain investments, such as mutual funds, to prospective investors. The prospectus contains information required by the SEC, such as investment objectives and policies, risks, services and fees.

Provider / Recordkeeping expenses

These expenses are a combination of various charges. Also

known as an asset management charge (AMC) or wrap charge.

Qualified / Nonqualified

These terms identify whether contributions are made with pre-tax or post-tax dollars. Qualified contributions come from money that hasn't been taxed yet, such as money withheld from your paycheck for your 401(k). Nonqualified contributions come from money that has already been taxed, such as the check you write for your Roth IRA.

Rate of return

The gain or loss on an investment over a period of time. The rate of return is typically reported annually and expressed as a percentage.

Real rate of return

The rate of return on an investment adjusted for inflation.

Redemption

The selling of fund shares back to the fund. This may also refer to the repayment of a bond on or before the agreed upon pay-off date.

Redemption fee

A fee, generally charged by a mutual fund, to discourage certain trading practices by investors, such as short-term or excessive trading. If a redemption fee is charged, it is done when the investment is redeemed or sold.

Return

The gain or loss on an investment. A positive return indicates a gain, while a negative return indicates a loss.

Risk

The potential for you to lose some or all of your investments, or to fail to achieve your investment objectives.

Risk tolerance

An investor's ability and willingness to lose some or all of an investment in exchange for greater potential returns.

Russell 1000® Index

An unmanaged index that measures the performance of stocks of the large capitalization segment of the U.S. equity universe.

Russell 2000® Index

An unmanaged index that measures the performance of the small-capitalization segment of the U.S. equity universe.

S&P 500® Index

An unmanaged, market capitalization-weighted index of 500 stocks of leading large-cap U.S. companies in leading industries; gives a broad look at the U.S. equities market and those companies' stock price performance.

Sales charge

A charge for buying an investment.

Sector fund

A fund that invests in a particular or specialized segment of the marketplace, such as stocks of companies in the software, health care or real estate industries.

Securities and Exchange Commission (SEC)

A government agency created by congress in 1934 to regulate the securities industry and to help protect investors. The SEC is responsible for ensuring that the securities markets operate fairly and honestly.

Security

A general term for stocks, bonds, mutual funds and other investments.

Separate account

An insurance company account that is segregated or separated from the insurance company's general assets. This also refers to a fund managed by an investment adviser for a single plan.

Share

A representation of ownership in a company or investment fund.

Share class

Some investment funds and companies offer more than one type or group of shares, each of which is considered a class. Examples include "class A," "Advisor" or "Institutional" shares. Each class has different fees and expenses, but all of the classes invest in the same pool of securities and share the same investment objectives.

Shareholder

An owner of shares in an investment fund or corporation.

Shareholder-type fees

Any fee charged against an investment for purchase and sale, other than the total annual operating expenses.

Sharpe ratio

Calculated using standard deviation and excess returns over the 3-month U.S. Treasury Bill to determine reward per unit of risk. The higher the Sharpe ratio, the better the fund's historical risk adjusted performance. The Sharpe ratio is calculated for the past 36-month period by dividing a fund's annualized excess returns by the standard deviation of a fund's annualized excess returns.

Single premium / Single purchase payment

A single premium annuity is a deferred annuity that lets you put money into your annuity account only once, when you first purchase the product.

Small capitalization (Cap)

Refers to either a small company stock or an investment fund that invests in the stocks of small companies.

Small-cap fund

A fund that invests primarily in small-cap stocks.

Small-cap stocks

Stocks of companies with smaller market capitalization. Small caps are often considered to offer more growth potential than large and mid-caps, but they may come with more risk.

Stable value fund

An investment fund that seeks to preserve principal and provide consistent returns and liquidity. Stable value funds include collective investment funds sponsored by banks or trust companies, as well as contracts issued by insurance companies.

Standard & Poor's 500® Index

An unmanaged, market capitalization-weighted index of leading large-cap U.S. companies in leading industries. This index gives a broad look at the U.S. equities market and the stock price performance of those 500 companies.

Standard deviation

A statistical measure of risk. It reflects the extent to which an asset's rate of return may fluctuate from period to period. When a fund has a high standard deviation, the predicted range of performance is wide, implying greater volatility. Morningstar computes standard deviation using the trailing monthly total returns for the appropriate time period. All of the monthly standard deviations are then annualized.

Stock

A security that represents an ownership interest in a corporation.

Stock fund

A fund that invests primarily in stocks.

Stock symbol

An abbreviation using letters and numbers assigned to securities to identify them. See ticker symbol.

Summary prospectus

A short-form prospectus that mutual funds may use with investors. A summary prospectus is used if a long-form prospectus and additional information is available online or on paper, upon request.

Target date fund

A fund designed to provide varying degrees of long-term appreciation and capital preservation based on your age or target retirement date. As you get older or closer to retirement, a lifecycle fund's mix of asset classes becomes less focused on growth and more focused on income. Also known as a lifecycle fund.

Target risk fund

A fund that maintains a predetermined asset mix and generally uses words such as "conservative," "moderate" or "aggressive" in its name to indicate the fund's risk level. Also known as a lifestyle fund.

Ticker symbol

An abbreviation using letters and numbers assigned to securities and indexes to identify them. See stock symbol.

Time horizon

The amount of time you expect to hold an investment before taking money out.

Total annual operating expenses

A measure of what it costs to operate an investment. These expenses are typically expressed as a percentage of an investment's assets, a dollar amount or in basis points. You pay these costs through a reduction in the investment's rate of return. See expense ratio and operating expenses.

Transaction-based expenses

Fees based on the execution of a particular plan service or transaction.

Trustee

A person or entity, such as a bank, trust company or other organization, that is responsible for the holding and safekeeping of trust assets. The trustee may have other duties, such as investment management. A trustee serving as a "directed trustee" is responsible for the safekeeping of trust assets but has no discretionary investment management duties or authority over the assets.

U.S. Treasury Securities

Debt securities issued by the United States government and secured by its full faith and credits. U.S. Treasury securities are the debt-financing instruments of the U.S. government. Often referred to as treasuries.

Unit

A representation of ownership in an investment that doesn't issue shares. Most collective investment funds are divided into units instead of shares. See share.

Unit class

Investment funds divided into units, instead of shares. Collective investment funds and other funds may offer more than one type or group of units, each of which is considered a class, such as "Class A". For most investment funds, each class has different fees and expenses, but all of the classes invest in the same pool of securities and share the same investment objectives.

Unit value

The dollar value of each unit on a given date.

Unitholder

An owner of units in an investment. See shareholder.

Value fund

A fund that invests primarily in stocks that are believed to be priced below what they're really worth.

Variable annuity

A variable annuity is a long-term investment product that provides a variable rate of return based on the performance of the investments you select. A variable annuity is a contract between you and an insurance company, and it's sold by prospectus. While it may take some time, you should read the prospectus. The prospectus describes risk factors, fees and charges that may apply to you.

Variable annuity charges

Variable annuities have fees and charges that include mortality and expense, investment management and administrative fees, contract fees and the expense of the underlying investment options. Variable annuities also have insurance-related charges, such sales expenses and surrender and transfer charges when an employee is terminated or withdraws from the plan's investment.

Variable return investment

Investments for which the return is not fixed. Variable return investments include stock and bond funds, as well as investments seeking to preserve principal but not guaranteeing a particular return. Examples include money market funds and stable value funds.

Volatility

The amount and frequency of fluctuations in the price of a security, commodity or market within a specified time period. Generally, an investment with high volatility is said to have higher risk because there's an increased chance that the price of the security will have fallen when an investor wants to sell.

Withdrawal

Also called a distribution, a withdrawal is the money you take from your financial account, such as an IRA. For retirement accounts, distributions made prior to age 59½ may be subject to a 10% penalty tax. All taxable distributions at any age are subject to ordinary income tax, and surrender charges may apply. You may incur fees or penalties when you make a withdrawal, depending on the type of product and whether the account is qualified or non-qualified.

Wrap fee

A fee or expense that is added to, or "wrapped around," an investment to pay for one or more product features or services.

Yield

The value of interest or dividend payments from an investment. The yield is usually stated as a percentage of the investment price.

12b-1 Fee

A fee assessed on certain mutual funds or share classes permitted under an SEC rule to help cover the costs associated with marketing and selling the fund. 12b-1 fees may also be used to cover shareholder servicing expenses. (Nationwide Insurance, 2019)

BIBLIOGRAPHY

Amadeo, K. (2019, May 11). *thebalance.com*. Retrieved from 2008 Financial Crisis: https://www.thebalance.com/2008-financial-crisis-3305679

Apple. (2019, June 18). Retrieved from Yahoo Finance: https://finance.yahoo.com/chart/ *Back To School Statistics*. (n.d.).

Back to School Statistics. (2019, August 07). Retrieved from nces.ed.gov: https://nces.ed.gov/fastfacts/display.asp?id=372

Barney, L. (2018). *Study Shows Low Level of Financial Literacy Among Americans*. Washinton, DC: https://www.plansponsor.com/study-shows-low-level-financial-literacy-among-americans/.

Beers, B. (2019, July 5). *Understand the What and Whys of Stock Splits*. Retrieved from Investopedia.com: https://www.investopedia.com/ask/answers/what-stock-split-why-do-stocks-split/

Burch, S. (2019, July 17). *Netflix Misses Big on Q2 Subscriber Growth, Stock Falls 10%*. Retrieved from The Wrap: https://www.thewrap.com/netflix-second-quarter-earnings-2019/

Burke, H. (2019, January 14). *How Many Ski Resorts Does Vail Own*. Retrieved from Snowpak.com: https://www.snowpak.com/news/how-many-ski-resorts-does-vail-own

Chart IQ. (2019, June 8). *Neflix, Inc.* Retrieved from Yahoo Finance: https://finance.yahoo.com/chart/NFLXChart IQ. (2019, June 8). *SBUX.* Retrieved from Yahoo Finance: https://finance.yahoo.com/chart/SBUX

Chart IQ. (2019, June 8). *Yahoo Finance.* Retrieved from Align Technology, Inc.: https://finance.yahoo.com/chart/ALGNDespres, R. (2019, January 17). *7 Most Common Stress-Related Health Problems.* Retrieved from Active Beat: https://www.activebeat.com/your-health/7-most-common-stress-related-health-problems/7/

Duggan, W. (2019, January 14). *Top Stocks to Buy in 11 Different Sectors.* Retrieved from Money.usnews.com: https://money.usnews.com/investing/stock-market-news/slideshows/top-stocks-to-buy-in-different-sectors?slide=13

Edesess, M. (2017, May 24). *Market Watch.* Retrieved from Opinion: Forget the fiduciary standard — financial advisers need a code of ethics: https://www.marketwatch.com/story/forget-the-fiduciary-standard-financial-advisers-need-a-code-of-ethics-2017-05-24

Fayed, A. (2019, June 12). *Quora.com.* Retrieved from How many times has the stock market crashed?: https://www.quora.com/How-many-times-has-the-stock-market-crashed

Feldt, E. (2007, November 9). *Visa Files for $10 Billion IPO.* Retrieved from Rueters: https://www.reuters.com/article/us-visa-ipo-idUSN0938404720071109

Finance, Y. (2019, August 7). *Dow Jones Industrial Average*. Retrieved from YahooFinance.com: https://finance.yahoo.com/chart/%5EDJIHagstrom, R. (2005). *The Warren Buffett Way, 2nd Edition*. Hoboken, NJ: Wiley & Sons.

Hagstrom, R. G. (2005). *The Warren Buffett Way (2nd Edition)*. Hoboken, NJ: John Wiley and Sons.

Herron, V. H. (2018, December 21). *The Sydney Morning Herald*. Retrieved from US stocks slide as government shutdown woes add to Fed angst: https://www.smh.com.au/business/markets/us-stocks-slide-as-government-shutdown-woes-add-to-fed-angst-2018

Kagan, J. (2019, June 25). *Estate Planning: W*. Retrieved from Investopedia.com: https://www.investopedia.com/terms/e/estateplanning.asp

Kagan, J. (2019, June 25). *Fiduciary*. Retrieved from Investopedia: https://www.investopedia.com/terms/f/fiduciary.asp

Keaton, W. (2019, May 4). *Investopedia*. Retrieved from Bernie Madoff: https://www.investopedia.com/terms/b/bernard-madoff.asp

Key Players in the History & Development of Intelligence & Testing. (2005, July 30). Retrieved from Wilderdom.com: http://www.wilderdom.com/personality/L1-5KeyPlayers.html#3&4TermanStern

Kiyosaki, K. (2019, April 4). *What is Financial Freedom?* Retrieved from Rich Dad.com: https://www.richdad.com/what-is-financial-freedom

Kiyosaki, R. (2008). *Increase Your Financial IQ.* New York: Business Plan Hachette Book Group.

Lynch, P. (1993). *Beating The Street.* New York: Simon and Schuster.

MacLellan, L. (2019, January 30). *The Countries with the Most Starbucks Locations.* Retrieved from qz.com: https://qz.com/1536009/the-countries-with-the-most-starbucks-locations/

Matthew Frankel, C. (2019, April 24). *The 100 Best Warren Buffett Quotes.* Retrieved from The Motley Fool: https://www.fool.com/investing/2019/04/24/best-warren-buffett-quotes.aspx

Milto, A. (2018, June 25). *Market Watch.* Retrieved from The fiduciary rule is officially dead. What its fate means to you: https://www.marketwatch.com/story/is-the-fiduciary-rule-dead-or-alive-what-its-fate-means-to-you-2018-03-16

Morning Star, Inc. (2019, May 31). *Kiplinger.Com.* Retrieved from Top Performing Mutual Funds by Category: kplinger.com

NASDQ.Com. (2019, July 30). Retrieved from What Are ETFs?: https://www.nasdaq.com/etfs/what-are-ETFs.aspx

Nationwide Insurance. (2019, August 7). *Nationwide.com.* Retrieved from Glossary of Financial Terms: https://www.nationwide.com/financial-terminology.jsp

Ong, H. (2014, May 28). *BusinessInquirer.Net.* Retrieved from What money lessons can we learn from the Jews? Read more: https://business.inquirer.

net/171575/what-money-lessons-can-we-learn-from-the-jews

Parker, T. (2019, February 1). *The Average Retirement Savings by Age.* Retrieved from Investopedia: https://www.investopedia.com/articles/personal-finance/011216/average-retirement-savings-age-2016.asp

Percardo, E. (2019, May 6). *Investopedia.* Retrieved from An Introduction to Dark Poolsx: https://www.investopedia.com/articles/markets/050614/introduction-dark-pools.asp

Purdy, C. (2017, April 25). *McDonald's isn't just a fast-food chain—it's a brilliant $30 billion real-estate company.* Retrieved from qz.com: https://qz.com/965779/mcdonalds-isnt-really-a-fast-food-chain-its-a-brilliant-30-billion-real-estate-company/

Puritz, S. (2019). *"Live Well and Retire with More".* Washington D.C. Metro Area: http://www.rebalance360.com.

Reiff, N. (2019, June 25). *Top 7 Companies Owned by Amazon.* Retrieved from Investopedia.com: https://www.investopedia.com/articles/markets/102115/top-10-companies-owned-amazon.asp

Robbins, T. (2017). *Unshakeable: Your Financial Freedom Playbook.* New York: Simon & Schuster.

Rose, J. (2018, December 5). *The New 2019 Federal Income Tax Rates.* Retrieved from Forbes.com: https://www.forbes.com/sites/jrose/2018/12/05/tax-brackets-and-rates-2019/#636af3353ec5

Segal, T. (2019, May 29). *Investopedia.* Retrieved from
   Enron Scandal: The Fall of a Wall Street Darling:
   https://www.investopedia.com/updates/enron-
   scandal-summary/

Shell, A. (2019, January 14). *5 ways empty nesters can
   boost their savings and turbocharge their 401(k)
   s.* Retrieved from USA Today.com: https://www.
   usatoday.com/story/money/2019/01/14/401-k-limits-
   savings-tips/2463677002/

Short, L. (2018, March 16). *Roe.House.Gov.* Retrieved
   from Roe and Foxx Praise Circuit Court of
   Appeals Ruling to Vacate Obama-era Fiduciary
   Rule: https://roe.house.gov/news/documentsingle.
   aspx?DocumentID=398300

Smith, E. (2011, September 19). *Netflix Separates DVD and
   Streaming Services.* Retrieved from The Wall Street
   Journal: https://www.wsj.com/articles/SB100014240
   53111904106704576579903892361530

Stanley, T. J., & Danko, W. D. (1996). *The Millionaire Next
   Door.* Atlanta, GA: Longstreet Press.

Tuchman, M. (2019, May 25). Here's what smart rich
   people really do with their nest egg. *Market Watch.*

Tuchman, M. (2019, April 13). Kevin O'Leary ... your debts
   paid off by age 45 . *Market Watch.*

Visa Files for a $10 Billion IPO. (n.d.). Retrieved from
   https://www.reuters.com/article/us-visa-ipo-
   idUSN0938404720071109

Webb, K. (2019, January 28). *5 Often Overlooked Tax Strategies as You Approach Retirement*. Retrieved from Kiplinger.com: https://www.kiplinger.com/article/retirement/T055-C032-S014-5-often-overlooked-tax-strategies-for-retirement.html

ENTEGRITY
CHOICE PUBLISHING

P.O. Box 453

Powder Springs, Georgia 30127

www.entegritypublishing.com

info@entegritypublishing.com

770.727.6517

www.ingramcontent.com/pod-product-compliance
Lightning Source LLC
Chambersburg PA
CBHW071555210326
41597CB00019B/3262